MW00527672

Passive Income Strategies to Build Your Wealth

Create Stability, Security, and Freedom in Your Financial Life, Second Edition.

Randy Wagner

1

Table of Contents

By reading this document, the reader agrees that under no circumstances is the author responsible for any losses, direct or indirect, incurred because of the use of the information in this document, including, but not limited to, errors, omissions, or inaccuracies.

ISBN (print Book): 978-1-955553-04-9

ISBN (Hardback): 978-1-955553-05-6

ISBN (eBook): 978-1-955553-00-1

Printed in the United States of America

Visit the author's website at: **www.randybwagner.com**

DOWNLOAD YOUR FREE GIFT!

READ THIS FIRST

Thank you for buying my book. I am giving you a unique free gift as a reward. You will find beneficial tips to budget your income 100% FREE

The free bonus gift will include the following:

-The guide of having a growth mindset to achieve your financial business goals.

-The best efficiency plan to set goals in your financial management.

-The importance of implementing the most valuable things in your business life and much more!

TO DOWNLOAD THE FREE GIFT! GO TO:

www.randybwagner.com

Follow me on social media!

@randywagnerauthor

@randywagnerauthor

Table of Contents

Contents

Table of Contents

Introduction

How would you like to leave your money problems behind and create a life of financial independence? I understand that most books of this kind begin with some variation of this line, and you might roll your eyes at that sentence, especially if you've read books on the topic previously and have tried to implement their advice.

No matter what your current financial situation is, whether you're broke or whether you can't seem to hang on to any significant amount of the cash you make, I'm here to tell you that a brighter financial future is there for you to grasp. Most financial advice falls flat on its face because the topic is attacked from a negative standpoint.

For example, when you read a book on personal financial management, the first thing you'll read about is budgeting or saving money, cutting expenses. Most gurus give you the standard advice to forego that expensive latte and drink water instead. Such advice assumes that you have no control over your spending or that you're a little child who needs constant advice on the most basic of tasks.

The truth is that most people that have financial troubles have their spending under control. The problem is that they don't make enough money to get over their problems. Someone who earns $1,500 per month after taxes is probably not spending money buying lattes every day if they have three mouths at home to feed.

Try telling someone who works two jobs that they should not spend money eating at restaurants when these visits are the only entertainment they can afford for their family. My aim is to adopt a more positive tone towards financial scarcity in this book. First, I'll help you understand why your mindset creates these issues.

Second, I'll walk you through understanding what passive income is and why earning it is so essential for your financial independence. While passive income is financial, its genuine power is realized through time.

Leveraging Time

Why do you want to be financially independent? You might answer by saying that you want to pursue your passions or spend more time with your family, or you might want to quit your job and travel for a while, and so on. These answers point to a common underlying desire: gain more control over your time.

Time is a resource that no one can earn more of. No matter how rich or how poor you are, everyone has roughly the same time on this planet. Money and luxuries are simply a way of buying more time for ourselves. Examine how pleased people live, and you'll notice that they do exactly what they want with their time. Your financial independence goal is tied intricately with how you wish to spend your time.

Your time has many demands on it. As wonderful as it would be to simply drop everything and do exactly what you want, you probably cannot do this without ruining your life immensely.

Therefore, you need to figure out how to get more done with your time.

As it relates to earning money, passive income helps you make more simultaneously as you usually have every day. It disconnects time from your ability to earn money. You can create as many income streams as you desire without worrying about how many hours you worked making them.

For example, working an hourly wage job is not a passive income source. Your salaried job is not a source of passive income. These income sources compensate you based on how many hours you worked or how much time you invested in the activity. Passive income doesn't depend on the number of hours you invest in creating it.

Don't mistake this for free income, though. You'll have to work for passive income and invest either time or money to create it. There is no free lunch or get-rich-quick scheme on offer here. You're going to have to work for your passive income. However, the degree to which you'll be rewarded for creating passive income is far greater than active income rewards you.

While active income requires a repeated time investment, passive income requires you to exert effort once. When enough passive income builds up, you won't have to rely on time to generate income. Your time will be your own, and you can choose to spend it however you wish.

My Story

So why am I writing this book? Why is it so vital that you realize your passive income dreams? I grew up in a pretty typical household and wanted nothing in my childhood. In fact, I always thought of my family as being rich. We always seemed to have luxuries around us, be it fancy clothes or cars.

I carried some of these habits into my adulthood but began realizing that I wasn't able to save much money living this way. I always assumed that my parents had enough money saved despite spending so much of it, so I figured I was missing something. I received a considerable shock when I realized my parents were broke!

Once they retired, they didn't have enough money to pay for their living expenses, and their nest egg was pitiful. Years of financial irresponsibility had jeopardized their retirement, and they forced me to look after them. During this time, I went back to the basics and tried implementing all the financial advice I'd already read about.

I budgeted, controlled my spending rigorously, avoided spending on lavish things, and so on. However, passive income boosted my financial position immeasurably. I'm not saying that you shouldn't focus on saving money. What I'm saying is that you need to save and make money as well.

The dual boosts that your financial status will receive will bring you close to your goal a lot faster. Fast is good. After all, this puts more time back in your pocket, and it's what you're after at the end of the day.

This book will detail all the methods that I have used with varying degrees of success to generate passive income. Note that just because some haven't worked for me doesn't mean you can't make them work for you. Everyone's different, and your strengths differ from mine. Therefore, take the time to read each chapter carefully and note how you can make a stream of income genuinely passive.

I'd like to remind you again that there is no such thing as a free lunch. You need to work hard to create passive income, and at first, it will seem as if you're doing a lot for no reward. Patience and persistence are the keys to making passive income. So be patient and trust the process.

After all, it worked for me and continues to serve me well. So, without further ado, let's jump right in and see what passive income means and how you ought to think about goal setting regarding the income you want to generate in your life.

Chapter 1: Introducing Passive Income

S o, what is passive income, and what's the big deal about it? Read any financial blog, and you'll see that term being thrown around as if it's a panacea. The truth is that passive income is massively misunderstood. It's both overestimated and underestimated—if that makes sense.

Many people chase passive income but unwittingly dig themselves into deeper financial holes. This happens because, to begin with, they don't understand what money is. They don't understand concepts such as debt and assets. They assume large amounts of debt and think the cash flow they receive is passive income. This might be true, but the passive income generated like this isn't worth it, and it won't put you on the path to financial freedom.

The true purpose of passive income is to help you achieve financial independence. Never forget this. Just because a stream of income is passive doesn't mean it's worth pursuing. You'll learn more about this as you progress through this book. For now, it's essential to understand that passive income disconnects time from the amount of money you can earn.

As I highlighted in the introduction, active income is tied directly to the amount of time you spent on an income source. For example, your day job is a dynamic source of income. You're expected to show up at a particular hour (no matter what your boss says) and to put in a certain number of hours every day. You're expected to complete a specific work quota, and you receive a salary in exchange.

The more time you spend at work, the greater your chances of promotion and the more money you'll earn. There's a misconception in the personal finance world regarding active income, especially when talking about financial independence. It's often painted as a bad thing or as something undesirable.

However, active income brings you the ability to generate passive income. It's a perfect thing, and demonizing it (no matter how much you hate it) is the last thing you should do. Sure, you might not like it, but there are many positive aspects. A much better way of approaching active income is to look at it as a stepping stone to better things.

Myths and Realities

Passive income is often pushed as a straightforward thing to create, but it's tough to make a sustainable source. However, the good news is that generating even a small amount of passive income will boost your wealth massively. Note that I'm talking about wealth, not cash or money. There's a massive difference between these terms.

Cash or money refers to how much you have in the bank to spend. Your bank balance is the amount of cash you have. Wealth is a more encompassing term that includes your net worth. It's a measure of the resources at your disposal. Your goal should always be to increase the amount of wealth you have. Cash is a part of your wealth, but it isn't all of it.

There's nothing wrong with having all of your wealth stored in cash. It's just that money isn't best used when it's in that form. It needs to be transformed into other formats (via investing) to generate wealth. Think of a situation where a person has $100,000 sitting in the bank as cash, while another has $20,000 in a savings account earning interest and $80,000 making them dividends through stock investment. At the end of the year, the former person has $100,000 intact. The latter has more money because their cash is working for them. In short, they're using passive income to boost their wealth. That's an outcome that everyone can get on board with! After all, who's going to say no to more cash.

A savings account is a great place to define passive income. You put your money in the bank, which pays you interest every year. You always have access to your money, and you can withdraw it at any moment. They claim the bank pays you every year to measure the amount of wealth you're generating.

The interest rate can also be called the yield. Yield is an important concept when talking about passive income. It can be defined as:

$$Yield = Cash\ flow/\ Principal\ invested$$

For example, if you've invested $10,000 in a savings account and pay you $50 every year, your annual yield is 0.005 ($50/$10,000) or 0.5%. Work is always expressed as a percentage. You can use it to evaluate different passive income opportunities. While everyone wants a high yield from their passive income sources, a high result isn't always a noble thing.

This is because yields can be boosted in various ways that increase risk massively. To better understand risk and its role, we need to talk about assets and debt.

Assets and Liabilities

The concepts of assets and liabilities originate from the business world and can get complicated in a hurry. From a personal finance perspective, it's enough for you to understand the spirit of them, as opposed to their accounting definitions. Accounting can often turn an asset into a liability, even when the object in question is an asset in spirit.

Briefly, an asset is anything that boosts your wealth. A liability costs you wealth. For example, a personal vehicle is a liability. It reduces in value over time (depreciates over time), and you can't sell it for more than what you paid for it. A property is usually an asset because it appreciates the time and increases your wealth.

Note that the definition of an asset or liability isn't dependent on the object's financial nature in question. For example, suppose someone who depends heavily on your personal vehicle to earn a living cannot carry out your duties without your vehicle. In that case, your vehicle is an asset despite it costing you wealth.

Let's say it costs you roughly $5,000 every year to maintain and run your vehicle. However, your vehicle allows you to earn $50,000 every year. If you were to get rid of your car, you'd save yourself $5,000, but you'd also be giving up $50,000 unless you found some other way of replacing it.

The value that something brings to your life can be qualitative, and it, therefore, becomes an asset. For example, you might love eating junk food once a week because it relaxes you and makes you feel good. There's no monetary value you can assign to this feeling, but it's safe to say that it brings you more value than the $11.99 it costs you to buy a meal.

Therefore, an asset's definition varies significantly from one person to another. A gym membership might be their most significant asset for one person, and they might be willing to spend large amounts of cash on it. For another, it might not be as big an asset, and they'd instead direct more money towards outdoor activities.

To figure out your assets, sit down and ask yourself what's important to you. Begin with the qualitative aspects first. Health is the most essential thing anyone has. Without it, no amount of passive income will improve your life. How can you keep yourself healthy, and which activities increase your health? The money you spend on these activities is being invested, not spent.

What are your liabilities? What are you spending money on that doesn't bring you value? Note that you can turn an asset into a penalty if you exceed spending limits. For example, you might need your car to carry out your work. However, do you really need a Tesla or a BMW 5 Series to do the job that a Chevy or a used Honda can do?

You cannot eliminate all liabilities from your life, but you certainly can minimize them. Buying a used car instead of a new vehicle is an example of reducing your liability. Paying for it in cash instead of drawing a loan is another example of minimization. To get wealthy and generate as much passive income as possible, you need to direct as much money as you can towards your assets and as little as possible towards liabilities.

Now that that's cleared up let's look at how assets and liabilities play a part in passive income yield.

Debt

Assets generate wealth. However, they can turn into liabilities that cost you wealth pretty quickly. An excellent example of this is property investing. Let's say you draw a mortgage and buy a home to live in. You're providing yourself a ton of security by guaranteeing yourself a roof over your head. You won't have to worry about rental payments or throwing money down the drain anymore. How true is this, though?

As long as you have a mortgage, you own nothing. The bank owns your home. Second, renting as throwing money down the drain is an example of how most people don't understand yields and return on investment. You need to think of investing money in terms of product at all times.

To occupy a property, you need to make mortgage payments and make an initial down payment. Let's say this sum amounts to

$26,000 in the first year. Your property's value will probably increase by (yield) 2%–3% on average over time. Note that this is an average return, not a yearly one.

If you could invest that $26,000 in an opportunity that yields you 2%-3% every year, are you generating as much wealth as you can? Probably not! Let's change this situation now.

Let's say you lose your job and cannot make mortgage payments anymore. The bank will foreclose on your property, and you'll lose your money. Was it worth assuming debt to buy the house in the first place? Probably not! When you draw a mortgage on a property, you think you can afford payments throughout the loan.

With a mortgage, this could be over 30 years. That's a long time to project. Note that this example applies whether you're occupying the property yourself, if your house hacking (renting out a portion of your primary residence), or investing in a rental property. You're assuming debt to generate cash flow (in the latter two options) and assume that you can make mortgage payments at all times. If you don't, you stand to lose a ton of wealth.

Get it right, and you'll make a lot. Using debt cuts both ways, as you can see. You can use it to boost yields immensely, but you also

Randy Wagner

risk losing a lot if you cannot make payments (called over-leveraging). An over-leveraged situation will destroy your wealth and will probably bankrupt you.

I'm not saying investing in property via mortgages is a wrong financial choice. Occupying property as a home can be a great asset for most people, thanks to the security they receive (a qualitative help). However, be careful when you use debt to inflate yields. You'll read about many real estate investors who claim they control $60 million in assets and that they built this empire in a few years.

They really have mountains of debt and assume that they can generate enough cash flow to cover interest payments. If the slightest thing goes against them, they'll be bankrupt. To control $60 million in assets, they've borrowed at least $48 million from the bank and have invested $12 million.

If they cannot make interest payments, not only do they lose $12 million, but they also dig themselves a $48 million hole. The decision to go ahead with this investment plan is to determine whether they can afford to take this risk. Most people can't. However, if the investor thinks they can cover this risk, it might work for them.

You should always consider the risk before looking at yields. High yields are typically a product of debt. Some forms of passive income generation, such as real estate, require you to assume significant debt levels. Taking on debt isn't bad if you plan to mitigate the risk of missing debt payments.

Don't go chasing high yields blindly. Always consider the risk in the situation and how sustainable the product is before putting your money into an opportunity. Always opt for the most minor trouble in a case, but don't try to engineer zero risks. You'll only end up missing great opportunities by doing that.

Time, Money, and Passivity

The time you spend directly shows how passive an income stream is. When thinking about passive income, most beginners dream of doing no work to generate large amounts of cash. This is a pipe dream. You need to put something in to receive something back. In the case of passive income, you need to invest either time or money (or some combination of the two).

Opportunities that are 100% passive always require money to be invested. For example, savings accounts or deposit certificates are passive income sources, but you need to invest money to generate a passive return. There's no work involved on your part other than putting your money into these sources.

A source such as rental income isn't entirely passive. You need to invest money, maintain the property, and manage your tenants. You can make tenant and property management completely passive by hiring a property management company, but you'll have to sacrifice yield to pay the company.

There's always a trade-off between time and money in every passive income opportunity. Technically, you can make almost anything passive. You could hire managers and employees to make nearly any income passive. However, will you generate enough yield over what this help will cost you? That's the question that most businesses grapple with when hiring employees.

You'll also have to face these trade-offs when you're thinking about generating enough passive income to live on. For example, let's say you need $5,000 every month after taxes to live comfortably (your goal). The average savings account with its 0.5% interest rate (a high yield account) will pay you $5,000 every month if you have $12 million invested in it.

This is a considerable sum, to say the least. A person who knows how to make that much money will presumably know better ways of investing it than sticking it in a savings account. Whatever your choice is, note that the savings account doesn't require you to do anything other than put your cash in it.

Contrast this with an online business that can bring in $5,000 every month. These businesses don't always require significant cash investments, but they need you to spend time on them. You'll find that generating this income is excellent, but you'll effectively work a second job maintaining it. Some people are okay with this, but this isn't truly passive income.

Over time, you can turn it into a passive income source, but most sources highlighted in this book require you to spend time building them before turning them into passive income sources.

Expectations and Goals

I'm highlighting these examples to help you develop the right expectations. Many people dive into passive income creation strategies with the thought that they can invest a small amount of money, a small amount of time, and generate enormous sums of money every month. It doesn't work that way.

You'll always have to put something in to get something back. Passive income takes time to develop, and you need patience. Passive income usually increases exponentially and not linearly. An example of exponential growth is a sum of $1,000 that increases 20% every year. In the first year, you'll receive $200. However, in the second year, assuming you reinvest the profit, you'll receive 20% of $1,200.

Our brains cannot comprehend exponential growth. So, we fall for get-rich-quick schemes since we cannot understand the role time plays in wealth generation. It's why we over-leverage ourselves since we think we need to make all the money in the world right now.

The fact is that there's a lot of time for you to make money. Work patiently at creating passive income streams, and you'll do just fine over the long term. Always manage your risks well, and you'll achieve your goals. So, what should your plan look like?

An excellent goal to target is to earn as much as it takes to live well. You can make this sum a monthly income or a yearly one. For example, if you need $5,000 to quit your job and live well, this is an excellent target to aim for. You could even think in terms of retirement. If you need that sum after the age of 60 to live well and maintain a high standard of living, start working with this book's strategies to create these income sources.

Understand that patience is your greatest asset. Keep doing the work, and over time, your passive income snowball will grow exponentially. That's when the real fun begins, and you'll have complete control over your Time and Money.

Chapter 2: Developing a Growth Mindset for Success

I t's no secret that your mindset determines the degree of success you'll have in your life. Whether you call it an abundant mindset or a growth mindset, the bottom line is the same. To achieve success, you need to think about it the right way. The question is: What is the right way to think about success?

Many books have been written on this subject, but there's no doubt that the common thread through all of them is that you need to work hard and challenge yourself to grow to succeed. This sounds easy enough to do, but the issue is that most of us have been taught the wrong things about success as we grew up.

How often have you heard of someone being called "talented" when they've achieved something? How often have you seen athletes on screen and have listened to announcers call them "genetic freaks" or "freakishly talented"? These phrases reflect a belief that success is a gene that some people are born with. The problem is that all of this is false.

Let's begin by examining that old bastion of talent, the intelligence quotient, or more familiarly, IQ.

Does Talent Matter?

Acclaimed psychologist Carol Dweck began her research into the psychology of success by unpacking what IQ is and how it's meant to be interpreted (Dweck, 2006). In her groundbreaking book *Mindset,* Dweck writes that its creator's IQ score was intended to be used as a marker of where teachers needed to focus more.

Alfred Binet, the score's creator, believed that IQ was malleable and that scores depend on context and testing mechanisms. He thought that any student's IQ score could be boosted with the proper training and environment. Needless to say, he didn't view IQ as something a person was born with. Instead, he used it as a test to determine comprehension and teaching effectiveness.

Binet repeatedly states that some IQ variation is expected in a classroom in his writings. However, significant variances in the

31

number point to ineffective teaching methods. This flies squarely against the way we view IQ scores. We look at someone who has a high IQ as a genius, and we classify mentally ill people as having a substandard IQ.

This misinformation has seeped so deeply into the education system that teachers unknowingly favor high IQ students and drill false beliefs into students perceived to have lower IQs. The lower IQ students believe they aren't born for success and that low grades are simply a fact of their existence.

These beliefs carry over to adulthood since lower IQ students never develop habits to succeed. Dweck mentions that one of the markers of success is the degree of work someone has put in to achieve it. In short, there is no shortcut to success. Talent does matter, but only in marginal situations. Mostly, if you want to go somewhere, you'll need to work to get there and grow throughout.

Talent as a Differentiator

I've just mentioned that talent matters. It's wise to explain how you can use it to push you further when it matters. The fact is that all of us are talented at something. Some of us are predisposed to recognize musical notes, while others are great at athletic pursuits. Some can concentrate for long periods, while others can memorize a ton of information without much effort (or less than those around them).

At the beginning of any activity, your degree of talent determines how much progress you'll make. If you happen to be innately talented at something, you'll progress further than someone who isn't. However, beyond a certain level, work is what determines progress. The qualified individual has to work just as hard as their competition to succeed.

Relying on their talent and neglecting hard work will cause them to fall behind. Combining skill and hard work cannot be overcome through sheer hard work. However, the differences are much more minor than you might think. For example, consider the former Olympic sprinter Usain Bolt.

He was freakishly talented and had dimensions that were unseen in 100-meter sprints. Bolt was an intermediate distance runner who transferred his skills to short races thanks to his genetic advantage. However, he had to work extremely hard on developing his skills. It isn't as if he simply showed up and broke world records. His competitors worked just as hard as him at the Olympic level; his talent was unique. However, he had to work to get there, and it wasn't his talent that took him all the way.

You see examples of this in top athletes all the time. The greatest quarterback of all time, Tom Brady, is far from being the most talented person ever to play the position. In fact, in his own generation, Brady is surpassed by several players' talent.

However, through sheer hard work, longevity, and dedication, Brady has willed himself to the top of his craft. Sure, luck has played a part. However, fate has been incidental to his career. His hard work stands out above all else. Michael Jordan and LeBron James, two of the greatest basketball players of all time, routinely talk about how hard they work at practice. You won't hear these high achievers talk about how talented they are.

This is because they know what talent is worth. It gives you a bit of a head start in life, but that's unsustainable without hard work. Contrast this to how most people treat success. They believe it should come to them quickly and automatically. We're in love with the idea of the child genius to whom everything comes automatically.

However, this flies against evidence in real life. Even child geniuses need to work hard. Mozart is often listed as the prototypical child genius. However, it's not as if he simply rolled out of bed and began composing music. He was predisposed to it but often spent his days writing, teaching, or practicing music. As per his letters in his early career, Mozart spent his days from 10 a.m. to 7 p.m. involved in some form of a musical composition or another (Popova, 2016).

As his career began to flourish, Mozart found himself sleeping for just five hours every night thanks to demands on his time. If the most talented individual of all time had to work this hard, what does that tell you about how much talent is worth?

Growing Through Work

Success directly results from growth, and growth happens when you surmount challenges. Challenges, for their part, occur when you work and keep moving forward. Therefore, the key to success works deliberately and challenging yourself as much as possible. Think of it as going to the gym.

The first time you visit the gym, you're unlikely to be able to lift much weight. You're going to be sore after your workout since your body isn't used to the stress. Over time, though, you'll lift heavier weight and be less painful since you'll grow stronger. The thing about success is that most people believe tasks get easier the more skilled you are.

This isn't true. The challenge remains constant. Objectively, a professional athlete's challenges are more significant than what a high school athlete faces. However, given their relative abilities, both sets of athletes need to work just as hard to overcome them.

Life will always throw challenges that get you to grow. Your challenges are perfectly tailored to help you grow and develop the skills you need to overcome them. Therefore, if you think your current challenge is formidable, give thanks for it. You'll likely experience a massive spurt of growth once you overcome it!

Of course, this is easier said than done. When experiencing a challenge, you'll likely feel as if the entire world is on your shoulders or that life is choosing you for its particularly tough challenges. Reminding yourself of the importance of the growth mindset will get you through these times. Visualizing your goal and feeling the positive emotions of achieving it when challenged are also great ways of overcoming your challenges.

Reframing Challenges

One of the best ways of negotiating challenges is to reframe them. If you've dabbled in self-help strategies, you're probably aware of the power of reframing. It's all about turning the problem on its head and viewing the positive aspects of it. For example, let's say one of your passive income ventures hasn't quite worked out, and you've lost some money on it.

The negative way of looking at this would be to mourn the loss of your capital and think you'll never make a success of this whole passive income thing. If you allow this train of thought to run uninterrupted, you'll soon begin visualizing pictures of never achieving your goals and so on.

When faced with a negative situation, always ask yourself if there's a positive way of looking at it. You could tell yourself that you've paid the price to discover what doesn't work in this particular example. Every setback has learning opportunities if you open your eyes to them. I'm not saying you should relentlessly practice this kind of thinking.

You're human, after all, and it's normal to get down on yourself. However, most of your thoughts should work in this positive manner, constantly reframing perceived negative situations into positive ones. Instead of approaching opportunities to make a success of them, look at them as learning opportunities.

Returning to our passive income example, you can remove the "need" to succeed by risking a sum of money that isn't all that important to you. Let's say you can replace $1,000 within a month through your active day job and will not miss that sum of money too much if you lose it. Obviously, you don't want to lose it, but you can easily replace it even if you do.

Establishing this framework allows you to focus on what needs to be done. Many people focus on the goal instead of what's in front of them. The result is they fall short and beat themselves up. It's great to set goals and to want to achieve them. However, you will get nowhere by looking at the scoreboard. You need to play the game the right way and execute.

Adopting an attitude of learning is a great way to set yourself up for a win-win. Not only are you risking an insignificant amount, but you're also telling yourself that whether you make this venture a success, you're still going to learn something from it. Again, I'd like to point out that this approach doesn't mean you're accepting things won't work out or that you're going to fail.

Instead, it adopts the growth mindset's attitude that learning and working is the way to get better. Focusing on the results is a limited mindset because it assumes that products come automatically. By adopting this mindset, you'll neglect the work that's in front of you and are going to sell yourself short.

Every time you're faced with a challenge, think of how much you can learn from a situation. This is opposed to the usual mindset of focusing on what might happen, whether you'll succeed or fail. The need to achieve (as opposed to wanting to achieve) places a huge mental burden on you. Every action of yours will be less potent because a part of your mind is always focused on looking at the goal and constantly evaluating whether you're close or far away.

Remove this pressure by focusing on what you can learn instead. This redirects your attention to the present moment, and you'll do a much better job. Ironically, you'll end up achieving what you want more often than not. Even if you don't, you've learned something new, so it's all good!

Delaying Gratification

The study of delayed gratification effects as they relate to success is fascinating. The most famous delayed gratification experiment was carried out by psychologist Walter Mischel at Stanford University in the 1970s (Mischel, 2014). As is often the case with the most exciting experiments, Mischel set out to measure one thing and ended up finding something else entirely.

Mischel's experiment aimed to measure the degree of self-control and impulsivity in children. Here's how he set up his experiment. A bunch of five- to six-year-olds were brought into a room one by one and sat down at a table. A desirable object such as a marshmallow, candy, or a toy was placed in front of them.

A researcher explained they could either interact with the desirable object in front of them or wait for 15 minutes and receive an additional hot object. For instance, if they waited for 15 minutes, they'd receive an extra marshmallow.

Some of the kids resisted while others gave in. Mischel didn't spot any significant patterns in this experiment, so he quietly put them away. However, during the late 1980s, he happened upon them again and was curious about how those kids got on in life. All of them were college-age or seniors in high school by that point, so there would be a decent set of indicators for how successful the kids were.

Mischel discovered a direct correlation between the success a child achieved and their behavior in the experiment. The kids who waited for 15 minutes and delayed gratification had uniformly higher SAT scores, were accepted into better colleges and reported greater happiness levels than those who couldn't wait for 15 minutes.

Upon further digging and experimentation, Mischel established a clear relationship between delayed gratification and the success a person can expect in life. Intuitively, this makes sense. Delaying gratification takes mental strength and focuses on the long-term benefits over short-term ones.

Focusing on the rewards in front of you at the expense of greater long-term rewards is a lot like being penny-wise and pound-foolish. Unfortunately, thanks to social media's rise, we're a generation raised on instant gratification. How often have you clucked impatiently as a website takes over five seconds to load?

Google notes that page loading speed is one of the most significant traffic volume indicators (Patel, 2019). There isn't more extraordinary proof of how we want everything right now, or preferably, yesterday. We've allowed companies to exploit our need for instant gratification and have reduced our capacity for success in return.

Instant gratification pushes you away from what's needed to achieve your desired success. You'll always focus on the result and will anxiously keep checking whether you've moved closer or further away from your goal. The product is a focus removed from the present action and guaranteed failure.

You need patience to achieve success. There's no way someone who is addicted to instant gratification will ever achieve it. Practice delaying gratification as you go about your day. If you want to buy something or indulge in something, try waiting for it for five minutes at first and slowly extend the delay. As you develop your gratification times, you'll notice that most of your desires are pretty weak and are energy drains.

You'll have more energy to direct towards your goals and work to attain them. The growth mindset in conjunction with delayed gratification is one of the best ways to achieve your desired success. It calls for discipline, patience, and consistent work. If all of those qualities sound terrible to you or undesirable, this is your instant gratification machine at work.

The growth mindset will protect you from falling for get-rich-quick schemes, and as you'll learn later in this book, the passive income generation world is awash with such tasks. Delaying gratification allows you to step back and rationally evaluate opportunities. It helps you avoid deciding when in an emotional swirl.

Marketing these days relies on exploiting our need for instant gratification. It pushes us into deeply emotional states by either scaring us or painting rosy pictures that simply cannot exist. Begin delaying gratification, and you'll escape the drug that is social media. You'll put yourself in a position to exploit it for your business and will end up generating the success you desire.

However, it all begins with recognizing the power of the growth mindset and the role patience plays. It's far easier to get rich slowly than to get rich quickly. So, take the simple route and adopt the growth mindset!

Chapter 3: Habits That Improve Self-Discipline

T o be patient and adopt the attitude of delayed gratification, you need to practice discipline. To most people, discipline is akin to being cooped up in a small, restrictive place. The average person thinks of discipline as a state of being where you deny many things to yourself. However, as you'll learn in this chapter, the field is what frees you to achieve everything you want in life.

The great news is that discipline is a skill that you can learn and develop like anything else. No one is born disciplined. It's a habit that you know from your environment and its people. Before diving into examining how you can build discipline, it's worthwhile taking some time to figure out how your brain learns information.

After all, if you're someone that needs to learn the habit of discipline, you need to know how your brain learns information!

How You Learn

Our brains are fantastic tools, but like any powerful tool, they can cause havoc when used in the wrong way. The best way of examining the state of your thought is to look around you and discuss your life. For example, if you've always desired riches and don't have any, your brain is working against you. It sounds simplistic to say this, but it's the truth.

Your mind gives you precisely what you want, on a deep level. By focusing on wealth, what you're doing focuses on the lack of it and, therefore, creates more incredible lack. The key is to learn positive habits that will push you closer towards the wealth you desire. Life will always give you lessons and opportunities to keep you moving closer. All you need to do is accept those lessons and learn them instead of imposing your narrative on events.

So how can you change the way your brain thinks? How can you gain greater control over your mind? Like everything else, learning how to use your thoughts to move you closer to your goals is a habit. If you've never used your mind to bring you closer to your goals, you've simply never had the opportunity to learn the information you need.

So, without further ado, let's look at how you can learn this information, any information for that matter, and form habits that support you.

The Pillars of Learning

Research has shown that there is a definite way to learn all the information you need (Hanson & Mendius, 2009). Habits are essentially pieces of information installed deep within your subconscious mind. For example, if you're someone who loves going to the gym and generally staying fit, this is because you have beliefs within you that frame yourself as someone reasonable and active.

The way to build such a view of yourself is to go out and repeat the habit as much as possible. Let's say you want to create a fitness habit in your life and want to be someone fit and healthy. Many people have this desire and make New Year's resolutions, but few manage to stick to them. Why is this? Simply, they don't repeat their desired habit.

To instill a new habit or learn further information, you need to do the tasks that reinforce your mind's knowledge. To get fit, you need to do what makes you fit. Sitting around thinking about it will not cut it. You have to repeat the information repeatedly until your brain gets it.

For a tool that's as powerful as our brains, it seems off that brute force repetition is the only way of learning additional information. However, that's how our brains are engineered. You literally are what you do every day. Be lazy and give in to your laziness by avoiding the gym, and you'll create a deeply held belief that you're someone who gives in to their momentary desires for rest instead of focusing on the long-term benefits of getting healthy.

On a biological level, repetition works because it creates neural networks within your brain that correspond to new information. More importantly, it helps you override old behavioral patterns that keep you in stasis. It's no accident that the more you wish to exercise, the lazier you feel, and the more sluggish your body becomes. Have you ever thought of exercising and suddenly felt lazy or felt a twinge in one of your joints?

This isn't an accident. Your existing neural networks are far more substantial than those that push you towards getting fit. All of this happens automatically, without conscious thought. However, by bringing awareness to these functions, you can consciously choose to practice new habits. You can remind yourself that your mind is playing tricks on you through its old neural networks and that you have the power to choose and repeat new ones.

The more you ignore old networks and their prompts, the more your brain gets the message that it needs to follow new behavioral patterns. One way of wrenching your brain out of its old neural networks and pushing it towards new ones is to use positive emotions.

Our brains prioritize emotions to a great extent. There's a reason people love watching horror movies or feel-good movies. They satisfy our need to feel emotions. Emotions help our minds become laser-focused. They remove all distractions, and your mind will have no problems identifying where it needs to focus.

Naturally, you want to use positive emotions to help your mind focus. You can use negative emotions, but why would you like to torture yourself? Think back to your negative childhood experiences and look at how they inform your current behavior. You'll see how powerful emotions can be.

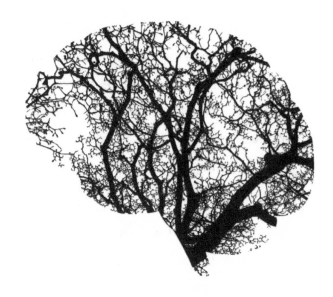

This is why setting goals and visualizing them is fascinating. The boost of positive energy you'll receive will help you focus on your goals and help your brain recognize the importance of what you're trying to achieve. Returning to the fitness example, by reminding yourself of why you must become fit, you'll feel a surge of positive emotions, and your brain will use that to override the pull of your old neural networks.

The point of using emotions to fuel you forward is to get your brain to focus. Focus is what you're after at the end of the day. Some people find setting fixed schedules helps them focus, while others find that a mix of play and loose scheduling helps them focus better. Do whatever you need to do to get your mind focused.

The focus is the third pillar of learning and repetition, and emotion. It helps your brain prioritize the task in front of you and enables you to direct your considerable resources efficiently. Working without focus is like running an Olympic sprint on one leg, with one arm tied behind your back. You can do it that way if you want to, but why would you?

You can use intentionality to boost focus. Your intentions behind completing a task are a powerful way of framing your guide. For example, let's say you're in the gym and are hit with a bout of laziness. Expecting the tricks your mind plays on you, you could tell yourself that it's your intention to finish your workout because you want to get fit.

Using your intention to permeate all of your actions is a great way to remain focused. Your purpose acts as a fence for your focus and helps it stay in place for more extended periods. Before you begin any task that's important to you, remind yourself of your intention, and you'll notice how focused you become.

To conclude, emotion, repetition, focus, and intention are the four pillars of learning. Along with these pillars, make sure your environment supports your growth. Surround yourself with people or objects that support you positively. For example, if you want to get fit, join a gym where people love working out and talk about getting fit completely. Don't join a gym where all everyone wants to do is pose in front of a mirror and take pictures for Instagram.

If you want to earn more money, participate in forums or talk to similarly motivated people. Don't spend your time-consuming information about how tough it is to make money or about how you need some secret key to unlock riches. Your environment helps you narrow your focus and drills within you the behaviors you need to succeed at your goals.

When setting out to achieve something, immerse yourself in it as much as possible. Don't take half measures. If you want to get fit, consume as much information as possible about training methods and start experimenting with what feels suitable for you. You'll find that once your brain gets the message, it'll assist you in your success.

With your mind by your side, you can achieve anything. Discipline, like anything else, is a habit. Start off by doing the tasks you need to repeat repeatedly. Build discipline into everything you do throughout your day.

Let's say you want to wake up at a specific time every day. Go ahead and do it. Set your alarm for that time, set a backup alarm, and set a backup to the backup as well. Before you go to sleep, set your intention to wake up refreshed the next day and do everything you can to ensure you sleep well. These actions won't guarantee that you'll wake up as intended the next day initially. However, carry them out over some time, and you'll find that your brain will automatically begin waking you up at certain hours, no matter what your sleep was like.

All of this habit building is great, but you need to direct it towards the things you want to achieve. This is where goal setting comes into play.

Setting Goals

Goal setting is an integral part of being successful. Unfortunately, most people do not know how to go about setting them. There are all kinds of goal-setting protocols, and all of them have intelligent-sounding acronyms. How useful they are is up for debate.

The fact is that goal setting has become overly complicated because most people don't understand a goal's function. A plan serves as motivation. It isn't a purpose. What I mean is that the key to achieving a goal is to enjoy the journey and focus on what you need to do next.

Instead, most people focus on the goal at all times and keep measuring their distance from it. This leads to a loss of focus on the current task, and the result is a failure. A goal is simply a destination. Your journey matters more than the goal. Think of it in terms of a road trip to a particular spot, and you'll get my point.

When you're on a road trip or are traveling somewhere, do you obsess over getting there? Probably not. You'd like to get there on time, but you also focus on doing what you need to do along the way. You make sure your car is fueled up, and you also make plans to take in whatever sights you happen to pass by along the way.

A singular obsession with reaching your destination will only result in you ignoring everything good about your journey. Incidentally, the journey is where growth happens. It's where you'll receive feedback for your efforts and encounter challenges. It's where you'll learn the skills you need to get to your goal.

Considering this information, how should you approach goal setting? The approach is quite simple. Begin by setting a goal that appeals to you. Don't worry about it being out of reach or too big or too small. The primary purpose here is to get excited. If your goal doesn't excite you, irrespective of its size, don't pursue it.

Often, we get caught up in chasing goals we think we are "supposed" to go after. Making a million dollars is a good example. Who says that a million is a worthy goal? If you're ambitious, a million might be too little. If you're someone who values other things in life, a million might cause you to overextend yourself when a lesser amount would do perfectly well for you.

Check in with your feelings and be honest about whether you're going after goals that excite you or whether you're chasing them because you feel they're the ones you "have" to pursue. Be true to yourself at all times, and you'll create goals that are meaningful and will provide you with the best opportunities to grow.

Don't get caught up in wondering whether they're time-bound or measurable or intelligent or whatever nonsense is written about goal setting. Your emotions are your best marker. If you're excited about a goal and feel good thinking about it, run with it irrespective of what someone else might think about it.

Charting a Course

Your next step is to start working towards that goal. This is where most people stumble. Thinking about a plan is excellent, but it's not worth much without action. Thought without action is a bit like dreaming of a vacation but never actually going on one. There isn't much purpose to it.

The first step you need to take will often be clear. It could be to learn more about something you need to master or to take action based on a decision you've made. What trips most people up is that they think they need to map out every step from the beginning to the end.

This is impossible to do. First, you don't know how many steps you'll need to take to get to your goal. It could be 100 or 1,000. Therefore, planning everything is a non-starter. There's also another reason you can't plan steps beforehand. Your goal excites you because it represents growth and expansion.

It represents a higher state of being and is outside your comfort zone. We're often told that we ought to set goals that lie outside our comfort zones. This is true. What we're not told is how to determine whether a destination lies in the right spot. Your emotions tell you this. Therefore, I made it a point to ask you to use your emotions as a marker previously.

If you're stretching yourself to an unknown point in terms of growth, how could you possibly know how to get there? If you knew how to get there, it implies you've been there already. If you've already been there, you cannot possibly be growing. Therefore, let go of the need to know all of your steps in advance. Instead, rejoice at you, not knowing how to get there.

This means you'll need to get creative and develop solutions that force you to grow. This is a perfect thing! As you execute your plans, you'll begin to receive feedback about them that you'll have to incorporate into your following actions. Step by step, you'll accomplish what you need to, and you'll find yourself at your goal before you know it.

Throughout, the key to your success is to keep focusing and doing what's in front of you. Do it with all of your focus and put as much mental energy into it as you can. Use your goal to motivate you when you feel low or exhausted. Never focus on it while completing your task at hand. If you work like that, you'll never finish anything.

Discipline is the key to ensuring you remain focused on what's in front of you. Building discipline is a habit, as you've already learned. Here are a few practices and activities that will help you build discipline in your life.

Building Discipline

The first habit that will help you become more disciplined is visualization. Visualization is a pretty easy habit of practicing. After all, you're already a master at visualization. Don't believe me? Well, think back to the last time you were plagued with worry. How did you behave, and what kinds of pictures did your mind conjure?

Most likely, worry ran ahead of you and painted terrible scenarios, all of its own accord. You most likely shrank away from these pictures, and the level of negativity in you grew. This is an excellent example of visualization, albeit one where you dreamed up negative scenarios.

Why not use it for positive purposes instead? Every day, set aside some time to visualize the positives in your life. Run through all of them one by one and start visualizing your goals. Feel the positive emotions run through you and use those emotions to power your actions.

Meditation is also a habit that helps you build massive discipline. Practicing meditation for as little as 10-15 minutes every day will help you focus your mind and set intentions effectively. Prioritize it, and you'll notice that you'll be able to bring greater discipline to everything else you do.

It's also helpful to schedule each and every minute of your day. I understand that this might seem to be overkill. However, when you schedule your day down to the last minute, it forces you to think in advance about how you'd like to structure your day and what you need to take care of. It prepares your mind for the next day and puts it in a goal-achieving frame of mind.

Take some time every night to plan your day ahead. Use a calendar to create blocks of time and plan everything out, including leisure and rest periods. Your mind will immediately switch to planning mode and start thinking of how it can be more productive.

Creating a schedule will also alert you to how you're spending your time every day and where gaps exist in your schedule. You'll become aware of whether you're spending most of your time working towards your goals or whether you're slacking off and focusing on things that aren't important to you.

When put together with the rest of the information you've learned in this chapter, you'll see that your discipline will increase by leaps and bounds. Set the right goals, focus on what's in front of you, and practice habits that build discipline using the right learning pillars. You'll manage to power your way forward faster than you can imagine.

Chapter 4: Stock Investment

W e're now officially in the "good bits" of this book. The previous chapters didn't directly address how you could build passive income, but they were necessary to put you in the right frame of mind. The principles of delayed gratification and long-term objectives over short-term ones are especially relevant when talking about the stock market.

The stock market these days often resembles a casino, unfortunately. This is sad because more than anything else, even real estate, the stock market is a place that can almost guarantee you riches. However, this doesn't mean these riches are easy to capture or that you don't have to work for them. It's just that with the right strategy, as described in this chapter, you'll generate tons of passive income without much effort.

Before jumping into the strategy that you can use to generate passive income, it's essential to cover a few basics about the stock market. Given that this isn't a book about investing in it, I cannot possibly protect all information regarding the market's nature. Instead, I'll be covering a few crucial principles you need to understand to invest successfully.

Let's jump right into the first one!

Rule One—Don't Lose money

This rule seems to be an obvious one and seems tough to follow. Well, the trick is not so much as to follow the law but to make sure you're doing everything you can to not break it. There are many consequences of following this rule so let's examine some of them.

First, if you've read anything at all about the stock market, you'll have read stories of how investors on Robinhood manage to earn hundreds of thousands betting on options and the like. You'll read about Tesla and other electric vehicle manufacturers and how they're "hot" stocks. You'll read about why this stock is making a comeback, why that stock is a dud, and so on.

All of this chatter makes it seem like the stock market is a game or a casino. The thing with the market is that it takes the shape of whatever you want it to be. If you treat it like a casino, you'll receive casino-like results. Who wins in a casino? Not the gamblers for sure! Some get lucky, but their performance is hardly repeatable.

When viewed in terms of the first rule of good stock market investing, you can see how the casino approach is in conflict. You're almost guaranteed to lose money if you treat the market like a casino. Therefore, don't. This is easier said than done because most market participants don't understand how to treat stock investment.

The simple answer is that you should treat your stock investments like a business. Always prioritize them and conduct investment operations along rational lines. This means doing your research thoroughly and understanding what you're investing in at all times.

It also helps to understand what drives market prices and how you ought to think about them.

Emotions and Rationality

Benjamin Graham is considered one of the greatest investors of all time because he was the first to articulate a rational approach to stock investment. Graham's exact methods don't work anymore because everyone is wise. However, his philosophy on the market remains timeless.

Graham famously said that the markets in the short term are voting machines, while in the long run, they resemble weighing machines (Graham, 1985). He was trying to say that emotions determine stock prices quickly. Some news item drops, and people rush to buy and sell stocks. Some CEO tweets something, and everyone runs to do what he says.

The financial media contributes to the hysteria by fueling trading activity and reporting everything breathlessly. Successful investors recognize that the actual substance only appears over the long term. A good analogy would be a person who constantly fools other people.

Over a short period, they might get away with hoodwinking others, but in the long run, the odds are pretty high that they'll be found out as people get wise to what their game is. Similarly, artificially induced moves in stocks will fizzle out over the long term since its intrinsic value will express itself in a long time. The intrinsic value is the value of the business that underlies the store.

This fact is something that most stock market gamblers forget to account for. Stocks aren't just pieces of paper. They represent real businesses that have earnings and employees. Looking at them as pieces of paper that fluctuate up and down is the wrong way to go about things.

Focusing on not losing money means you need to make sure you've done everything you possibly can to minimize your chances of losing money. This means thoroughly researching what you're getting into and understanding it inside and out. The fact is that the average person is ill-equipped to understand a business inside and out.

After all, it's not easy to understand a sector's economics and how market conditions will affect a business's future prospects. All of this is before we get to accounting methods and interpreting financial statements. Even if someone can make sense of them, it's unlikely they'll have the time to decipher them.

Therefore, for most people, investing directly in stocks is inadvisable. You'll lose money more likely than not. If you're investing in something that you don't understand, you're breaking the first investment rule, so don't do it.

Rule Two—Always Have a Margin of Safety

The margin of safety is an engineering concept that Graham borrowed to explain sound investment principles. The margin of security or safety factor is pretty easy to understand. When engineers design bridges and buildings, they make a ton of estimates about material stress and strain limits.

These limits are not meant to be 100% accurate since it's impossible to estimate them. The problem is that if you make enough estimates that are slightly off, you're building a lot of error into your final design. To mitigate this risk, engineers finish their calculations and multiply the result by a factor (say 1.5 or 2) to account for errors.

It's a simple technique. Doubling your calculated result ensures you'll build a lot of safety into your design. Even if you misestimated something, you would manage to guarantee security since you'd create a massive buffer into the design. Regarding investing, the margin of safety is applied in both your investment operations and the way you approach the question of capital.

First, the best way of making money in the market is to remain invested for the long term. You've already learned why this is the case. To stay supported for a long time, you need to ensure you don't touch your investments or withdraw them. Therefore, you need to invest money that you don't need to pay your bills and daily expenses.

Don't invest money that you'll need down the road for a down payment or anything else. Always have enough money saved up for emergency expenses. Do not need to touch your investments to pay for them. Create a buffer around your investment capital so that you're almost guaranteed to remain invested in the market for as long as possible.

The Investment Process

How can you build a margin of safety around your investment process? For starters, you can implement investment methods that satisfy the first rule. By making sure that you don't do things that lose you money, you'll put yourself in a position to make money automatically.

This means you need to let go of the need to get rich quickly. As you've already learned, this results from your need for instant gratification and is unlikely to lead to success. Instead, you need to be patient and invest in the right opportunities. More importantly, you need to understand the options you're investing into.

You need to also make sure that you're realistic about the amount of time you have on your hands to generate your desired returns. It's tough to create above-average market returns. To do this, you need to invest significant amounts of time. Most people don't have this time since they work full-time jobs and have other demands to fulfill.

There's also the fact that your objective with stock market investing is to generate passive income. If you're spending all of your waking hours trying to make money from stocks, then you're not generating passive income, are you? Trying to beat the market is an active pursuit.

Therefore, your objective should be to minimize your time spent worrying about your investments and to simply stash money into them and have them make you money. By reducing the amount of time spent worrying about your assets, you're reducing your chances of doing something silly and sabotaging your long-term view. In other words, you're building a margin of safety around your investment operations.

The Best Strategy for Passive Income

I won't beat around the bush with this. The best way of generating passive income in the stock market is to invest in dividends. A dividend is a cash payment that a company makes to its shareholders. Usually, dividends are paid from the profits a company makes. I say "usually" because there are some exceptional cases thanks to the emotional way the market views tips.

While companies aren't obliged to pay dividends to their shareholders, those who do tend to be viewed more favorably than those who don't. They are regarded as more stable companies, and in the long run, tend to hold their value better through market downturns.

The flip side is that these companies are usually so large that they don't have much room to grow. Therefore, they aren't fast growers. For instance, Amazon has never paid a dividend, and neither has Google. However, if you've invested a portion of your portfolio in companies that are fast growers, you can dedicate the rest of it to dividend stocks and funds.

Picking the right dividend stock is a challenging task. This is because of the same reasons as I previously mentioned. It's tough to analyze a company's business and to evaluate what its prospects will look like in a few years. The goal of passive income is for your money to make you money without you having to spend too much time monitoring it.

Therefore, the best way to generate passive dividend income is to invest in dividend index funds.

Indexing

An index is a collection of stocks that fulfill specific criteria. For instance, you can create an index of stocks that begin with the letter X, or you could make an index of stocks that are active in the airline sector. There is no end to the number of indexes you could create. Whether anyone would follow them is another matter entirely. Usually, large and reputable financial institutions such as Standard & Poor's (S&P) and Moody's create indexes according to various criteria.

The S&P 500 is an index that has existed in its current form since the 1950s. It aims to capture the cumulative stock performance of the 500 largest companies trading in the American stock markets. As a result, while the American economy has changed since the 1950s, the index itself hasn't suffered.

If anything, it has accurately captured the growth that American companies exhibited from the 1950s onwards. This is because the index's criterion is simple. It only screens in the largest 500 companies by size. If a company's prospects decline, and it falls out of the index, it's replaced by a new company. In the 1950s, steel companies and chemical manufacturers dominated the index.

These days technology and finance companies dominate it. While individual company prospects have varied over the years, the index has always risen because the American economy has expanded. In fact, research shows that the S&P 500 has returned an average of 10% every year since its inception (Graham, 1985).

How great would it be to invest directly into an index like this? The problem is that indexes aren't tradable instruments. The only way to invest in an index is to invest in an index fund or an indexed exchange-traded fund or ETF. These funds replicate the index's stock holdings in their portfolio and thus capture the index's performance.

Some indexes screen dividend-paying stocks. The most famous of these is the Dividend Aristocrat List, which screens all companies that have steadily increased their dividend payments for the past 25 years. Companies such as Coca-Cola and Johnson & Johnson are prominent members of this list. Coca-Cola has increased its dividends for over 50 years.

The other famous dividend index is the Dividend Achievers List, maintained by NASDAQ (the stock exchange). This list screens in companies that have increased their dividend payouts for over 10 years. It's more growth-oriented than the Aristocrats List since the period is shorter. The Achievers List companies have room to grow but aren't precisely early-stage companies.

Choosing the Right Funds

You can follow other dividend indexes, but the issue is that there aren't any low-cost funds that track them. You want to minimize costs since they can eat into your return over the long run. Stick to funds that charge less than 0.1% of assets as fees every year.

Pay attention to the fund size as well. Choose funds that are over $10 billion in size since this gives you an idea of how reputable it is. Look for managerial stability and check whether the fund accurately represents the underlying index. The fund will trail the index a bit since it incurs trading fees. However, this gap shouldn't be more significant than 1%.

How Much Can You Make?

Right, it's time to address the critical question: How much money can you make investing in dividend index funds? The average stock index fund yields around 2%–3%. A real estate investment trust (REIT) index fund yields around 5%. REITs manage real estate and transfer 90% of their profits (earned via property management) back to shareholders.

You could invest in REIT index funds and earn higher yields. However, you'll be exposed to the vagaries of the real estate markets entirely. It's best to split a dividend portfolio in a 70/30 ratio between stocks and REITs. This means your theoretical yield will be around 3%. A $100,000 investment will yield $3,000 per year or $250 per month.

Of course, not many people have $100,000 lying around. Stock investing is a safe and utterly passive way to generate passive income, but the flip side is that you'll have to invest a lot of money to compensate for the complete lack of work. It's best to allocate a portion of your income every month to a dividend investment portfolio and keep buying over time.

Remain invested for at least 20–25 years, keep reinvesting your dividends, and you'll have enough to retire with at the end of that period. This is because you'll also experience capital gains during that time. Given that the stock market rises by an average of 10% every year, an investment of $12,000 every year over 25 years will result in an ending principal of $1,180,164.

Assuming you earn 3% of that ending portfolio amount in dividends, you'll make close to $3,000 per month entirely passively. Increase your investment horizon to 30 years, and you'll end up with close to $2 million. Three percent of that is $5,000 per month in passive income.

It takes time to generate sizable passive income through dividend investing. However, the rewards are worth it. Remember the lessons about delayed gratification and keep investing. Over time, you'll make enough so that you never have to work ever again.

Chapter 5: Rental Income

While not as passive as dividend income, rental income is a great way to build passivity into your earning streams. There are different ways of earning rental income. The broadest ways are through your vehicle and property investing. The former doesn't need much money and is a great way to reduce your liability burden.

The latter requires considerable money and time investment, but it's a great way to boost your net worth and earn cash flow at the same time. Let's begin by looking at how you can monetize your vehicle.

Car Rental Income

Unless your vehicle is central to your business and active income, it's probably a liability. It costs you money every month, and it depreciates in value over time. You need to pay insurance for it, and once your loan is paid off, you'll realize that it's worth far less than what you paid when adding back interest.

The fact is that the average car loan is underwater. This means that most people end up owing more on their remaining car payments than the car is worth. If you draw a loan to buy a luxury car, you can definitely expect to be underwater within three years.

Yet, a vehicle is a necessary evil (financial evil). You cannot drive around in a beater since that's hardly going to do the job for you. Any decent vehicle will cost you money, and it can be tough to scrape together the five figures it's going to cost you. Ideally, you'll want to pay as much of it upfront and minimize the impact interest has on the overall amount you pay.

However, if you could find a way to generate income from it every month, you could theoretically have your car pay itself off. There are two ways of generating rental income from your vehicle. The first is to rent it out, and the second is to offer it to advertisers.

Renting Your Car Out

How great would it be if you could rent your car out to travelers and have them return the keys to you once they're done with it? Well, this is what services such as Turo and HyreCar promise. There is a slight difference between the types of people these services rent your vehicle out to.

Turo offers vehicles on its platform to pretty much anyone who signs up. They could be a recreational driver or professional ones. HyreCar rents your vehicle out only to rideshare drivers. This means your car will be used by Uber and Lyft drivers. There are pros and cons to this that I'll shortly explain.

There are other services such as GetAround and TravelCar, but Turo and HyreCar are the biggest and highest-rated services on Trustpilot (a global business review website). The way these vehicle rental services work is quite simple. You sign up for an account and post pictures of your car along with availability times. Given HyreCar's ridesharing focus, you'll have to list your car for longer times than on Turo.

Your car's make and model also determine how much money you'll make. Turo renters are generally more recreational in nature and prefer desirability over practicality. This means a

BMW will probably be more popular than a Honda. The opposite is true with HyreCar since rideshare drivers are looking for an economical means of transport.

Therefore, if you have a dependable car, you're probably better off choosing HyreCar. Once your vehicle is booked, you'll get the opportunity to meet and evaluate your renter. You can approve or deny them based on your evaluation of them, and assuming everything is okay, you hand your keys over to them.

Once their rental period is over, you collect your car back from them and note any damages or issues you find. If there are none, you approve the delivery, and that's all there is to it. You get to keep the rental fee in almost every case unless the renter finds significant issues with the way you described the car (*5 Ways to Make Money Renting Out Your Car*, 2021).

HyreCar offers industry-leading rideshare insurance to cover any damages about insurance. Turo offers up to $1 million liability coverage. The catch is that Turo sets thresholds for cars that qualify for their platform. Your vehicle needs to have less than 130,000 miles on it and must have a market value of less than $150,000.

Turo offers classic car rentals as well. The criteria are a maximum value of $85,000 and a make older than 1990. Obviously, your car needs to have some classic car appeal. Listing your old Prelude is unlikely to bring too many enthusiasts flocking to you.

Both of these services pay out on time, and you can expect to earn anywhere from $300 to $1,000 per month from them. Obviously, a lot depends on your car's appeal and the number of hours you can spare it for. HyreCar tends to payout higher earnings on average, but this is because of its rideshare focus.

Note that while earnings might be potentially more significant, you'll put more miles on your car through them. There's also the fact that your car will be used as a taxi, and there are greater chances of something going wrong, especially if you plan on leasing it at night to ferry people during the typical bar-fighting and Doner kebab-seeking hours.

Advertisement

While renting your car out is the primary income method that strikes most people when talking about using a vehicle to make money, a better way to generate passive income is to use your vehicle as a billboard. Brands are always looking for better ways to reach their audience, and a vehicle that travels through an inevitable part of town regularly is an excellent way for them to get their customers.

Services such as Carvertise will help you turn your vehicle into a rolling billboard. The advertising option is a much better one than renting your car out since it's truly passive. You won't have to give up control of your vehicle to a stranger, and you don't have to drive additional hours to earn money. Simply do what you usually would and let the money roll in.

Carvertise's platform connects you to companies looking for ad space, and the amount of money you'll earn depends on the miles you drive as well as the location you're in. For obvious reasons, those living in metro areas will make much more than those living in rural areas. Other factors include whether your car will be placed in mostly uncovered parking areas or covered ones (visibility) and the time of the day it'll be on the road.

You might dread rush hour traffic, but advertisers will pay you more for it if your car is a billboard. On average, Carvertise states that vehicle owners can earn anywhere from $100 to $500 US every month. If your car payment is around $300, including insurance, that's a great deal.

Carvertise takes care of everything for you. You'll have to drive your car to a local detailing shop where it'll be wrapped in the company's advertising. Typically, campaigns last for a month or so. Once the month is up, you'll drive to the shop again to have the detailing removed.

Note that both of the methods I've highlighted won't make you rich overnight. In most cases, your vehicle is a liability, and the thing to do is reduce its burden on your finances. These methods of passive income generation will help you reduce that burden. It's possible to scale your efforts and turn it into a business in renting your car. However, a company isn't a passive income generation machine.

You'll need to work hard to maintain it. In effect, you'll be running a car rental business, and that's not a passive income generation method even if you hire a manager. So, make sure you're comfortable with the degree of activity you're experiencing with these methods and choose an appropriate level for yourself.

Rental Properties

Rental properties are the most talked about sources of passive income. However, it takes time to make property investing genuinely tolerant. For the most part, you'll have to work hard to set things up so that you can make it passive someday. In the beginning, be fully prepared to be a full-time landlord.

You'll often read that you can turn property investing into a passive activity by hiring a property management company. This is theoretically true, but it doesn't work well in practice since you won't maintain your property standards. I'll explain why this happens shortly. For now, let's dive into the world of property investing and see what it's all about.

Sourcing Rentals Properties

There are two broad categories of properties you can look at when investing in rentals. The first is a turnkey rental, and the second is a rehab project. A turnkey rental is a ready-to-rent property where you can start earning cash flow once you sign the papers. In most cases, turnkey properties will have tenants present within them.

A rehab project is what most beginners to real estate think about when talking about property investing. The idea is that you buy a run-down property, spruce it up, and rent it out. You'll capture a price increase as well as cash flow by doing this. However, this method is rarely suited for beginners since you might end up biting off more than you can chew.

The best kinds of rental properties lie somewhere in between turnkeys and rehabs. They're properties that need some basic sprucing up, like a coat of paint, some appliances reinstalled, and furnishings upgraded. The capital gains increase won't be much with these properties, but you'll be able to lease them for a significantly higher price than what was initially listed.

The best easy to find these properties include driving around your neighborhood, using online sites such as Roofstock or Zillow, and contacting a local real estate agent. When working with an agent, remember that they work for the seller, not you! This doesn't mean they'll push you into terrible deals, but they're not exactly concerned about what you do with the property either. To them, everything they show you is a bargain.

Chapter 5: Rental Income

Attending your local real estate investment club meetups is also a great way to get in touch with people in the area. You'll meet contractors and other investors who can help you understand the basics better. You'll need to work with these people at some point, so make sure you network with them.

Math is essential when it comes to evaluating the worthiness of property investment. Thankfully, it isn't tough to figure these numbers out. First, you want to focus on the rental yield. Remember the formula for a generic product from the first chapter? Well, this formula isn't all that different:

Rental yield = Annual rent earned / Property purchase price

When looking at a property, yield is the number you want to focus on first. Note that most online listing sites and property professionals will quote the gross yield to you. The gross yield doesn't take into account maintenance costs and other expenses. The net yield is what you'll actually earn because it takes those expenses into account. Here's an example that illustrates the difference.

Property price = $100,000

Annual rent = $12,000

Annual maintenance and expenses = $6,000

Gross yield = $12,000/$100,000 = 12\%$

Net yield = ($12,000-$6,000)/$100,000 = 6\%$

As you can see, there's a big difference in this case between the gross and net yield. A net profit of 6% is quite good in many areas, to be fair. However, compared to the gross profit of 12%, it's not as enticing. You'll be lured into deals by the gross yield, so watch out!

When choosing a property, it's wise to aim for at least 12% gross yield. This means the annual rental income needs to be at least 12% of the property's listing price. Some real estate investors quote this as the *one percent rule*. This rule states that the gross monthly rental income has to be at least 1% of the property's value.

It's the same 12% yield rule framed differently, so don't get confused by this. It's easier to calculate 1% of a number than to figure out what 12% is. So, use whichever formula works best for you and apply that. Remember that the one percent rule applies to monthly rentals, while 12% refers to annual rental income.

This rule helps you figure out how much you should offer for the property. You can quote a lower offer price to bring the property up to match the one percent rule, or you can consider investing in the property and add value to it, thereby increasing rent.

A few ways of increasing rent include improving the curb appeal (landscaping, paint, etc.), offering amenities such as pet-friendly living, fully furnished units, and so on. You can also add accessibility ramps and increase the rental price. Customizing your team for seniors is also a great way to increase rent.

The key is to find a niche in your area and use that to boost value. Note that there are trade-offs here. You'll have to spend money to make money. Adding accessibility ramps is an expensive undertaking, and while pets improve your tenants' quality of life, they also leave huge cleaning bills you'll have to deal with.

Financing

Financing is the most essential part of a real estate deal. You'll have to deal with a lot of paperwork, but the best thing to do is to be prepared beforehand. Before you move on a property or even locate one, approach a lender and apply for preapproval. The lender will give you a letter that states how much you can expect to borrow from them at what interest rates.

Having this letter in hand when approaching sellers is like having a superpower. The seller will instantly treat you better since they know you're serious and that you won't have to undergo lengthy approval times. You'll also save a lot of time by not hunting for properties you don't have a chance of financing.

A good option for many investors is to choose Federal Housing Administration (FHA) financing (Scott, 2015). FHA financing requires lower down payments (usually 3% to 10% of the property's value) and offers lower interest rates in some cases. However, the FHA stipulates that the borrower must live on the property to qualify.

You can finance a multiunit purchase and live in one unit while renting out the others. This way, you'll always be on the premises to deal with issues. Note that none of this is passive at first.

Chapter 5: Rental Income

There's no way to entirely turn property investment into a passive activity unless you have a significant roster of properties.

If you have at least four or five properties, you can afford to hire a manager and have them run the daily activities. However, you need to pay this person a decent wage to keep them motivated. You can't pay them out of the rental income you receive on one property. You could hire a property management company, but they bring their own headaches.

For starters, these companies have hundreds of properties they're looking after. Your single property isn't going to move the needle too much when looking at their bottom line. They're unlikely to prioritize your property, and you run the risk of alienating your tenants. A good quality tenant will not stand for a property that isn't maintained on time, and you'll end up attracting poor quality tenants who never pay on time and create all kinds of problems.

So, prepare to be a landlord with your first few properties. Alternatively, you could invest in a multiunit property to get more units under your belt and be treated seriously by property management companies.

Earnings

So how much can you earn from property rentals? A lot depends on the individual deal. However, you want to aim for at least a 5% net yield. Estimating maintenance and operational expenses is the most challenging bit for new landlords. A good rule of thumb is calculating expenses as 50% of your rental income.

This means, if you earn $500 as rental income per month, you'll spend $250 every month maintaining the place. Note that you won't pay this amount every month. However, it's a good idea to keep this money aside for emergencies. Your property will lie vacant sometimes, and this is an expense as well. Always set aside 50% of your rental income in your bank account to pay for these lean times.

Some landlords unwittingly underprice their rental rates. How can you figure out what's appropriate? The easiest way is to look at rental listings in that neighborhood for similar properties. Alternatively, you could speak to local real estate professionals and ask them what the cap rate is. Cap rate is short for capitalization rate and is calculated as follows:

Cap rate = Rental income per year/ Market value of property

Note that this formula is similar to that of the rental yield. However, the yield takes the purchase price into account, while the cap rate takes the current market value into account. These numbers will differ over time. The great thing about the cap rate is that it removes the need to look for similar properties when determining rental prices.

All properties in a neighborhood will usually have similar cap rates. If you note that the average neighborhood cap rate is 4%, and you're generating 6%, you know you're doing pretty well. So always keep the cap rate in mind when you price your rentals. You'll leave money on the table if you ignore this.

Storage Rentals

A close cousin of property investing is storage rental investing. Many property investors prefer this kind of investing since there aren't the usual maintenance issues to deal with, and it's easier to create a passive income stream from such properties. However, many unscrupulous sellers have used this theme to trick beginner investors into buying useless storage units.

Here's the unvarnished truth of storage rental investing: You need to buy an entire lot to generate real passive income. You cannot buy one or two units or even multiple units within someone else's lot and hope to create a steady income. This is because storage units generate real passive income. Well-maintained storage units attract long-term tenants.

More often than not, these units' owners have no desire to sell since it's easy money for them. It's the owners of terribly maintained storage properties that advertise, using the passive income angle. What happens is that their units are lying vacant, and no one wants to lease them.

Therefore, they pass the risk on to a beginner investor who hopes to earn a passive income. Instead, what happens is that the owner finances the sale of the unit and gets paid a monthly amount in cash (plus interest from financing). At the same time, the investor sits around hoping their company receives a tenant.

Even if the property owner undertakes massive advertising, your units are not their priority. After all, they're already earning rental income from it. They're more likely to push tenants towards the units they aren't making cash flow from. As a result, you get the short end of the stick.

So always choose to invest in an entire lot. Don't buy individual units. Sure, there might be stories of people succeeding by investing in these things, but they're rare. Investing in the entire lot, adding value to it, and running it the right way is the key to generating passive investment income from these properties.

Choosing the Right Property

Genuine storage rental bargains are hard to find. More often than not, you'll find that the best deals lie in existing storage yards that are poorly maintained. A storage yard's ideal location is somewhere near a major traffic intersection, preferably close to businesses requiring warehouses, such as car dealerships or furniture shops.

You'll often find them a few miles away from downtown areas and the suburbs. When scouting locations, look for signs of poor management. This includes a lack of advertising (both online and offline), the lack of proper management presence, and the general lack of maintenance on the property.

It's a good idea to pose as a prospective renter to scout places out. Pay attention to how well you're treated by the staff on site. If you don't find a team onsite during working hours, you've probably hit the jackpot since there's a ton of value to be unlocked. Search for "storage rentals near me" on Google and see which ones show up. Now check whether they're in good condition or if other yards aren't showing up.

Occasionally you might end up finding a place that is in good shape and has an owner that wants to sell. This is a dream scenario for you, but don't hold high hopes for it. The easiest way to add value to an existing property is to install new management, install the right software to track rentals, and clean out delinquent units. Impose strict rules and regulations, along with proper security infrastructure, and you'll generate excellent cash flow from the yard.

Financing

Financing is a tricky thing with storage yards. However, if you can arrange it, it's a great deal. The trick is, to begin with, a bridge loan. A bridge loan typically lasts for a few years, usually under five years, and gives you the financing you need to stabilize operations and bring the business into profit.

If you've taken over a poorly run yard, then you can use bridge financing to get things in order and bring occupancy rates over 80%. Once you've done this, you can refinance with a traditional lender, such as a bank, and continue to run the property. You'll need a bridge loan to stabilize the property since banks won't finance a renovation or a rehab.

Another option is to approach a conduit financier. Finding these people is tougher since they don't exactly advertise their services. However, you can find them by networking with existing real estate investors.

Is It Passive?

This is the big question. Is all of this passive? As with traditional real estate, it isn't at first. You'll have to put a lot of work into stabilizing the business. However, once it is up and running, and as long as you have good managers and processes, you can earn a good amount of passive income.

Note that this is a business, so it's not as if you can set and forget it like dividend investing or a savings account. However, it's a great way to divorce your time from the money you earn, which is the key to generating passive income.

Chapter 6: Pay Off or Reduce Your Debt

When speaking of passive income, the average person thinks about making money without working. However, one key to increasing the amount of money you have leftover at the end of every month is to reduce your debt. To put it in another way, reduce your cash outflow while maximizing your cash inflow.

There are many demands on your cash and wallet. You need to pay rent, utilities, vehicle payments, and so on. I know I spoke about avoiding any talk of budgeting in this book, but I want to introduce you to a different way of thinking about how you spend your money in this chapter.

Most talk of budgeting and reducing debt is negative. Legal advice tells you to sacrifice and let go of many of the things you'd like to have in your life. However, this is a miserable way to live, and it's no surprise that most people struggle to get rid of debt or maintain financial discipline with such tactics.

The trick is to figure out what you value and use your budget to propel yourself towards financial freedom. If you've been reading legal, financial advice, this might seem incongruous. After all, isn't a budget a way to deny you the things you want? Before we look at how you can use your budget to build the life you want, let's look at the mindset you need to have first.

Value Versus Price

Everything you consume in your life has a price attached to it— even the things you don't pay for. For example, the time you choose to spend with people who inject negativity into your life costs you down the road. You could have spent that time building up your self-image in positive ways and could have figured out better ways of taking action to improve your life. Instead, you spent that time beating yourself up and reinforcing old negative habits.

The key to getting ahead is to gain more value from an activity than what you pay. If you keep investing your time and money on things that give you more value than what they cost, you're going to come out ahead, eventually. It's just plain logic. Imagine buying everything for 50 cents on the dollar, all the time. You'll save a ton of money.

This doesn't mean you try to haggle and buy everything at a discount all the time. I'm not talking about spending habits here. I'm talking about something that is at a higher level than that. Your philosophy in life should be to invest your time and money in things that bring you as much value as possible.

Everyone values different things. I might love chocolate cake every Friday, while you might prefer a cinnamon roll. Everyone's different. One person might like to live in a swanky apartment and drive a beater car. You might prefer minimizing housing expenses and spending more on entertainment.

There isn't a single way of describing what's valuable and what isn't. It's different from one person to the next, and this is why traditional budgeting methods fail. They tell you to stop eating out and stop eating that avocado toast every morning. Skip the fancy lattes and drink homemade coffee instead, they say.

Well, that's no way of getting rich. It's true that if you don't really like or value the fancy latte, it makes no sense to spend money buying one. However, you definitely have the intelligence not to spend money on things you don't like. Why would you buy a seven-dollar cup of coffee if you don't like it?

You're not some infant that doesn't know how the world works. What you instead need is awareness. You need to be aware of how good something makes you feel when you possess it. This is where many people trip themselves up because they confuse short-term, feel-good vibes with long-lasting feelings of satisfaction.

The Difference Between Feeling Good Now and Long-Term Satisfaction

Our generation has been raised on social media, and our instant gratification senses are off the scale. We want everything now, without question, as you've already learned. However, as you've also known, prioritizing the long term is far more beneficial for our lives.

What feels better? A shiny extra pair of shoes or a vacation with your family? If the boots are fancy enough, both those options might cost the same. I'm not saying that it's wrong to buy fancy shoes. In some situations, buying the shoes might be the better long-term choice. If you've saved for many years, and are buying them as a reward, then good for you!

However, if you're buying them to serve some short-term desire, such as wanting to post about it on social media or gain appreciation from those around you, it's not a wise choice. One of the world's wealthiest people, Warren Buffett, often describes himself as an inner scorecard guy (Schroeder, 2009).

Buffett uses the inner versus outer scorecard concepts to describe his life values. He's routinely been one of the five wealthiest people in the world since the mid-1990s and lives in the same home he purchased back in the 1960s. He drives an ordinary sedan to work and doesn't have a team of bodyguards surrounding him around the clock.

He doesn't live in New York or Paris, but in Omaha, Nebraska. He pays himself a hefty salary of close to $200,000 every year. However, when you consider that he's worth close to $100 billion, that amount of money is a pittance. Buffett lives by his inner scorecard, and he's pretty happy by all indications.

So, what's your inner scorecard like? What are the elements that it's composed of? An excellent exercise to figure out your inner financial scorecard is to ask yourself how much money you need to make every month to not worry about it. Some people need to make $5,000 per month to forget about money issues, while others need to earn $7,000.

Research shows that the average American adult would forget about their financial burdens if they earned $75,000–$80,000 every year (Hoffower, 2021). That's far less than the millions and billions all of those internet gurus tell you to make! This sum is so low because it considers the fact that you won't spend money on things that you don't value.

Being rich isn't about making tons of money. It's about having money left over at the end of the month once you've paid for all the things you value. Some liabilities might be valuable to you. Your car might be a liability, but if you love to wake up every morning and look at that gleaming piece of metal, who's saying you're wrong to buy it? If you can afford it and minimize its impact by earning cash flow elsewhere, how can it be a burden to you?

Sticking to your inner scorecard makes you happy. If you spend money on the things that bring you happiness, you're unlikely to feel inadequate or as if you're wasting money. Many people earn over a million dollars every year but have nothing left over at the end of the month. This is because they spend money on ex-wives, empty mansions, expensive schools for their kids, and fancy cars. Other than the education expense, nothing else is precious.

Always check with your inner scorecard to see whether you're investing your time and money the right way. Your inner scorecard will always point you toward long-term value, so always heed its advice.

Getting Rid of Debt With Your Budget

Chapter 6: Pay Off or Reduce Your Debt

Now that you've learned about the inner scorecard and have thought about how you can better spend your time and money, you're in the perfect position to create a budget that will power you towards financial freedom. There are two sections that you need to have within your budget.

The first is your necessary expenses, and the second is your financial freedom category. Let's look at them.

Necessary Expenses

Necessary expenses are those you have to pay to live every month, like rent/mortgage payments, utilities, vehicle payments, insurance (medical, dental, life, vehicle, home, etc.), and debt payments. Debt is the big one here and is what trips up most people. The average American carries a massive debt burden these days (Hoffower, 2021).

Most financial advice is catered towards reducing debt, and most of it is correct. Merge your debt as much as possible, avoid creating new debt (credit cards, mortgages, etc.), and pay off the highest interest debt first in a cascade. This is the waterfall method, espoused by Dave Ramsey's financial expert, and it really works (Hoffower, 2021).

Interest kills you with debt since it's a wholly avoidable expense. Of thumb, never pay interest and avoid it like the plague. I'm not saying you should break the law and not pay interest. It's just that you should avoid paying for anything that has interest attached to it.

The only exceptions are property investments that you can generate cash flow from. You can use the cash flow to reduce the impact that the debt payment makes on your overall financial position. Assuming debt to live in a house and not generate cash flow from it makes no sense and is an example of bad debt.

You can use an app or a spreadsheet to track your expenses every month. This is a matter of discipline more than anything else. You should log your receipts or categorize your expenses correctly on your app. Many personal finance apps such as Mint connect to your bank account and help you create thresholds and spending categories.

Remember to spend money on things that bring you value. You'll find that these things are often cheap and straightforward. For example, a stroll through a park at sunset is free. A single ice cream cone is unlikely to be expensive after a strenuous day. Minimizing meals at restaurants is also an excellent practice to follow.

Don't eliminate all forms of leisure. Instead, work them into your budget. Treat entertainment and "blowing off steam" as a necessary expense. Schedule it and treat it with all the importance of the world. Your budget isn't a punishment tool. Use it to help you feel better and plan your expenses beforehand.

If you know that a dinner and a movie will cost you too much, then figure out how you can reduce that expense. Perhaps you could eat dinner out and stream a movie at home? Or you could rent a movie with a one-time payment? These days, there are many options, so do your research and choose the one that makes monetary sense for you.

Financial Freedom

The point of a budget is to help you get your money working for you. It's no good to keep your money sitting silently in your bank account. It needs to earn returns or interest for you to benefit. The financial freedom categories will help you figure out how close you are to your desired goal (your inner scorecard monthly earnings).

If you have any form of debt, you should not be contributing to these categories. The benefits that these contributions will have will be erased by the interest you'll have to pay. Therefore, it makes sense to eliminate debt as fast as possible and then turn your attention to these categories.

It's a tough pill to swallow for some, but this makes the most sense over the long term. Once your debt is eliminated and is at manageable levels (such as low credit card debt that you can instantly pay off), you can turn your attention to building financial freedom.

The first and most clear of these categories is the emergency fund. It always pays to have a backup. Make sure you've saved at least six months' worth of living expenses in your bank account. It's best to stick this money in an interest-bearing account easily accessible.

This means you should choose a savings account that doesn't have a minimum balance or take a few days to give you access to your cash. Many high-yield savings accounts impose minimum balances and don't give you immediate access. What you could do is break up the emergency fund and deposit one month's expenses in a regular savings account. You could then deposit the remaining five months' expenses in a high yield account.

Once your emergency fund is built, you can turn your attention to investment. This means investing in the stock market through a retirement account or an employer-funded retirement account. Make sure you take full advantage of the matching plans that your employer gives you. It's literally free money, making no sense to decline it.

Many employers contribute up to 20% of your deposits. Make sure you deposit as much money into those 401(k) as possible and keep investing in divided indexes to boost your passive income gains. Best of all, these will be tax-free, so keep reinvesting and keep getting that free money from your employer.

You might also want to set up a business fund. Many passive income opportunities require an initial sum to be invested before they can really get going. It's a good idea to save around $4,000

in an interest-paying bank account to take advantage of any passive income business opportunities that might arise.

Last, you also want to contribute to any category that is important to you. Take a dream vacation or learn a new skill (fly-fishing, scuba diving, etc.). It could even contribute towards a down payment on a property. Whatever it is, contribute to the things you value and keep directing money towards them.

Over time, you'll have enough money saved up in different accounts and will have a wealth of possibilities to direct your resources towards. You'll be earning passive income from your portfolio as well as receiving free money from your employer in that account. You'll have an emergency fund that will keep growing thanks to the interest it earns every year. You'll have money to take advantage of any potential business opportunity that can generate even more passive income for you.

It all begins with being disciplined enough to contribute money via your budget every month and being patient. Your budget lets you know whether you're hitting your goals, so keep track of it and immerse yourself in it. It's your tool to achieve financial freedom.

Chapter 7: Network Marketing

T hose who can market and sell will never lack money. These days, thanks to the explosion of online resources, it's easier than ever to sell products and earn commissions from them. This doesn't mean you can snap your fingers and expect sales to come pouring in. It doesn't work like that, unfortunately. However, you can expect to earn a good amount of passive income with some work.

The primary ways to earn money through marketing are affiliate marketing and network marketing. The first is an online venture, while the second can be offline or online. Network marketing often gets a bad rap thanks to pyramid scheme operators' preponderance in that business line.

However, there are legitimate network marketing schemes you can take advantage of. Before we look at them, let's dive into affiliate marketing and see how you can generate passive income from that.

Affiliate Marketing

Affiliate marketing is one of the simplest ways of making money online. Here's how it works. A company needs to sell its product online and generate as many sales channels as possible. It incentivizes people via sales commissions to direct traffic to their product's page. The salespeople are paid a commission based on how many clicks they produce lead to sales.

In this scenario, the company is the merchant, and the salesperson is the affiliate. Often, there's another party involved in between these two called the affiliate marketplace. A marketplace is where affiliates and merchants come together. In the old days of affiliate marketing, the primary way of sending traffic to a product page was via a website or blog.

Someone would blog about a topic and list a few helpful links to products. For example, you could blog about dog training and leave a few links to leashes, treats, and so on. If people bought those products, you'd earn a commission. Amazon is one of the most prominent merchants and affiliate networks globally. That it carries every known product to man in its catalogs means that there' are plenty of opportunities to earn affiliate cash.

Many big retailers have affiliate programs as well. If you're interested in fashion, you could start a blog and monetize it by leaving affiliate links to stores like Asos, Amazon, NET-A-PORTER, and so on. Using blogs to generate affiliate income is excellent, but it isn't an entirely passive income source.

You'll have to spend a lot of time creating content that excites your readers and needs to invest time and money into drumming up traffic. If the topic you're blogging about doesn't interest you, then you're dead in the water. It usually takes a year and a half to generate enough traffic to earn money.

However, if the topic interests you, you're knowledgeable about it and are focused on providing value first, you'll succeed. The amount of money you could earn through affiliate commissions varies based on the products you're selling.

Typically, digital products pay far greater commissions than physical products. Courses and so on usually pay you 50% commissions. If you manage to refer people to web hosting products such as Bluehost, you'll earn high one-time commissions and monthly recurring income.

However, much like chasing high yields with dividend stocks, don't chase high commissions just for the sake of them. Always figure out where you can add value and begin there. Creating content is an excellent way of ensuring a steady stream of income over the long term.

Note that you can create written as well as video content. YouTube is an excellent resource to leverage in creating content. There are so many support systems out there that help you create videos for a low price if you're not comfortable appearing on camera.

You can use whiteboard software or animation software to create engaging videos to bring in a ton of views. The key is to add value, as always. Don't create videos in something just because you think you can make a lot of money from it. Value comes first. If people don't value what you have to say, they will not give you any money.

Social Media

Social media is a necessary evil in our lives these days. If you have to use these platforms, why not use them to make money? Facebook, Pinterest, Instagram, and Twitter can be affiliate money machines if you do the right things. Let's begin with the biggest of all platforms, Facebook.

While it's a valuable platform to generate political vitriol, Facebook has a feature that other social media platforms don't. Groups are precious things on Facebook, and you can use them to generate affiliate commissions. Note that Facebook doesn't allow you to post affiliate links on its platform. You'll have to create a web page or a website and direct users there first.

You can use your website's affiliate link to direct people to the product page. However, this method takes far less time than creating a website from scratch. If you can contribute to discussions within these groups properly and recommend suitable products, you can generate a lot of money.

For example, home furnishing groups are full of people looking for product recommendations. If you have a single web page that lists a few of your suggestions with affiliate links, you can post the link to your web page on Facebook and direct traffic there. If people like your recommendations, they'll click your affiliate links and buy the products.

Instagram is also a great way to direct affiliate traffic. However, the issue is that you can post just one link on Instagram in the account description section. This limits your ability to earn affiliate income. Also, growing an account is tricky and time-consuming. Instead, what you could do is pay an existing account and ask them to post your link in their description. This link could be to your website that contains affiliate links.

Affiliate marketing through Twitter also works the same way. Pinterest is the only platform that allows you to post affiliate links directly within your pins (images). Each forum has its own quirks, so take the time to study them and figure out what works.

Despite these methods' cheap nature, note that value still comes first. People aren't going to randomly buy your product just because you spam them with links. You'll have to provide value and show that you know what you're talking about. Without that, there isn't any way you can earn affiliate income.

Choose your niche carefully since it makes all the difference. Don't be worried about saturation or competition in a place. The online world is enormous enough for many people to make money. However, there are two niches that you'll need to have qualifications for to make an impact.

These are medical niches and finance. Even personal finance niches are highly competitive, and all companies screen content creators for credentials. For example, if you're offering personal financial advice, you need to have certificates to rank high in search results.

Those experts you read about who don't have financial credentials benefitted from being early movers in the niche. You don't have that advantage, so don't think you can replicate their business model. Stick to niches you're interested in, want to explore, or have a lot of knowledge about.

Don't begin by looking at product commissions and choosing niches based on that. Affiliate marketing is a harsh method to put into practice, and it takes time. If you aren't prepared to wait for at least a year before receiving significant income, then it's probably not going to work for you.

Multi-Level Marketing

The mere mention of multi-level marketing (MLM) sends people into a panic, thinking they're dealing with fraudulent schemes. If you've never heard of an MLM scheme before, here's how it works. A company wishes to sell its product to people and hires a few people to sell the product. It pays them commissions based on how many products they sell and how many people they sign up to the MLM network.

However, they set terms that these people need to buy vast quantities of the product as part of their membership in the MLM scheme. These initial members turn around and sell products to other people (called they are downstream) and sign these people up to membership in the MLM.

These second lines of people repeat the process with others, and gradually, the network expands. At some point, the network becomes too saturated for anyone to make money selling the product. This is where the fraud begins. People aren't aware of how low they are in the pecking order, and they sign people up with hopes and dreams.

However, product sales aren't enough to compensate these people, and as a result, fraud accusations grow. The only way people can now earn money is by signing up other members. At this point, a responsible MLM will step in and stop offering memberships. Irresponsible ones will eventually get flagged by the US Federal Trade Commission (FTC) and shut down.

So, is it possible to make money through MLM schemes? The answer is complicated. For starters, the entire business model rests in a gray area. People are compensated based on how many members they sign up to the network and the number of products they sell.

An intelligent person will quickly understand that it's easier to sell the promise of passive income to people than selling actual products. After all, you'll earn a cut of all the commissions your downstream earns. For example, if you sign up for one person and sign up two people, and those two people sign up a further two each, you'll earn commissions from seven people.

At that point, you won't need to do any work since you'll make more than enough from your downstream commissions. If you've done your homework and have signed up to a good network, you'll earn commissions from product sales as well. However, since the bulk of your commissions come from signing people up to the web, it's safe to say that the closer you are to the top, the better.

What to Watch Out For

There are a few telltale signs to watch out for MLMs. First, look at the number of people that are upstream from you. If there are over three people, it makes little sense to sign up. Unfortunately, most MLM schemes that offer placement within them will have more than this number of people.

If you have over three people upstream, this means there isn't enough room for you to grow your network and sign up enough people. After all, the three people above you have been signing multiple people up as well. The network at that point would have grown exponentially, and you'll be reduced to signing up your family members and friends.

That brings me to the next point. Do not sign up your family members and friends to these schemes. It's best not to involve them in any business transaction that could go wrong since you'll lose money and the relationship. You'll also put them in a tough spot since they'll find it hard to say no to you. If the MLM company pushes you to sign them up, then walk away since that's a good indicator that you're too far downstream to make any actual money.

Check out the products that the company offers as well. Are they well made, and do they have any scientific claims backing their efficacy? The scientific claims bit is significant because many of these schemes push alternative medical products on people, which can land you in boiling water if you aren't careful. Besides the potential legal claims against you, you might also find yourself branded a nutter, which is never a good thing.

Last, look at the network's quality and what their events are like. Many of these networks host cult-like gatherings and try to push their members' get-rich-quick schemes. You'll be manipulated into believing that you're signing up for the best thing since sliced bread and that there's no way you can ever fail.

The problem is that most people in an MLM will fail. So, watch for false propaganda of this sort, and don't let your emotions run away with you.

Chapter 8: Income From Selling Books

What if you could pen an influential book and then sit back collecting royalties from it for the rest of your life? That's the dream, anyway. However, thanks to a wide variety of publishing outlets these days, it's more than possible to earn passive income from book publishing.

The largest and most influential book publishing resource is Amazon's Kindle Direct Publishing (KDP) platform. KDP was the first to arrive on the scene in a big way, and despite a few hiccups early on, it's a legitimate way to earn passive income these days. I must mention that many courses out there teach you how to generate passive income from self-published books.

Some of these courses are legitimate, while the vast majority are outdated and fraudulent. Watch out for any period that promotes methods against Amazon's service terms. Most of these methods involve review manipulation by paying people to leave you favorable reviews on your book listings.

In the earlier days of KDP, these methods worked very well, but Amazon's algorithm has become sophisticated enough to spot these techniques. It will push your book listings down passively if detected. Instead, it's best to approach the whole thing to build your brand slowly and steadily.

Self-publishing a book is perhaps one of the most mysterious ways of earning money passively. It isn't suitable for most people since not many people can write engagingly to warrant a book. You'll hear a lot being said about hiring ghostwriters to create books for you as a means of "automating" book creation, but this is nonsense.

A high-quality ghostwriter will charge from low four figures to high five figures to write a book. If you're looking to hire writers from Upwork or Fiverr to create your readers, then you're probably going to receive a plagiarized piece of work. A few writing companies out there have varying reputations, but these can be hit or missed.

The monetary investment makes achieving truly passive income an arduous task in the book publishing business. The best approach to adopt is to cut costs as much as possible and maintain quality. Hiring a writer is going to make that impossible to do. Therefore, if you can't write a book yourself, it's probably not going to be a viable option for you.

I'm not saying it's impossible. It's just that the business's economics these days mean that it's tough to spend that much money and earn passive income. Most people making a lot of money are holdovers from the early days. They've built a sales track record with Amazon, and their new books are instantly promoted.

However, new accounts don't receive this treatment and are often penalized if sales don't dramatically increase. After all, all Amazon cares about is the number of sales it can make.

Niches

The most important decision you'll make regarding your publishing business is your niche. Like most online businesses, choosing a good niche will make your life a lot easier. The most popular niches on KDP are self-help books about making money and productivity books. Cookbooks and financial books are popular, but they are pretty competitive. Fiction niches are pretty popular, and I'll address them shortly.

With KDP, selecting your niche is just the beginning. Keyword research plays an important role when deciding which books you want to publish. Thankfully Amazon makes your life easy regarding figuring this out since they post every book's Best Seller Rank (BSR) on the product listing page.

The lower the BSR is, the better the book has sold. For example, a book with a BSR of 100,000 sold fewer copies than a book with a BSR of 50,000. A book's BSR fluctuates depending on its own sales and its competitors. Like everything else, the key to finding success on KDP is to identify niche topics (keywords) with low competition and many best-selling books.

Many books with BSRs less than 100,000 are considered a reasonable threshold. The greater the number of books under this threshold, the more profitable that keyword is. The trick is to limit your focus to keywords with low competition, which is a bit more subjective.

Evaluating Competition in Nonfiction

You can use a few tools to determine the competition you're facing with a keyword. The first is the number of reviews a book has. A trendy book is going to have many reviews. Mainstream book publications have upwards of 500 reviews.

A less popular, self-published book will have between 50-100 reviews if it sells well. Less popular books that are self-published might even have no reviews. The number of reviews decreases over time since Amazon deletes older reviews automatically. It also deletes any review it deems false or against its service terms.

The next indicator of competition is the number of results the keyword brings up. Search for appropriate keywords, navigate to Amazon's Kindle Store and type phrases related to your niche. You'll see Amazon suggests several keywords for you. These keywords are what most people are searching for, so make a note of all of them. Search every one of them individually.

When starting off, it's best to limit yourself to keywords with less than 1,000 results. The fewer the results, the better. A low number of products shows that there aren't too many people publishing under that keyword. If all the books showing up for that keyword are selling well, with the majority of BSRs under 100,000, and if the number of reviews is low, you have a potential winner on your hands.

It's also a good idea to check when the books were published. If the majority of books in that keyword category were published within the past six months, it's a sign that more people are jumping on the bandwagon, and your ability to stand out is going to decrease. Often, specific keywords become popular at times, and the number of results increases exponentially.

You could see a keyword give you 500 results, but within a month, that number can jump to 2,000 thanks to the emerging popularity. Stick to keywords that haven't seen much activity over the past six months. As long as most of the books have been published outside of that period, it's an excellent keyword to operate with.

Lastly, pay attention to the authors showing up in the results. For example, if you were to search for value investing, you'll receive a low number of products but books that have been authored by investing legends. There's no way a self-published book will stand out in this niche. Amazon penalizes new books for poor sales quite a lot. This means even if you manage to land in the first spot for that keyword, if your sales aren't good enough, you'll find your book demoted to the second or third page within a few hours.

To summarize, look for keywords that return results under 1,000, a large number of books with BSRs under 100,000, a low number of reviews (preferably under 50), no recognizable authors, and nothing published in the past six months.

Finding Keyword Ideas

A particular problem most beginners run into is finding good keyword ideas. The most popular keywords will often be inundated with competitive titles, and it can be hard to find good keywords. You can use a few techniques to mine keyword ideas in such instances.

The first is the alphabet soup method. In this method, you type your prospective keyword in the search bar and follow it with the letter a. For example, if you're searching for a suitable keyword beginning with value investing, you should type in *value supporting a.*

This will give you a few suggestions in the search bar. Next, type *value investing b* and so on until you *value investing z.* This method will yield a good number of potential keywords to further explore. Not all of them will be winners since some might not make sense. However, it's an excellent way to spark a few ideas.

Another great place to look for keyword ideas is to examine the subtitles of published books. Mainstream published books won't have long subtitles. However, self-published books look to leverage Amazon's algorithm as much as possible, and you'll see many keywords stuffed into their subtitles. These keywords often prove to be winners since there's a reason the publisher included them in their subtitle.

Take a look at the book descriptions since they usually include a few keywords. Collect all of these keyword ideas together, and you'll have a decent list to explore further.

Fiction Niches

Fiction keyword research works a bit differently. Here, instead of searching for keywords, you're looking for tropes and themes. For example, romance and science fiction are broad themes. Within these themes, you'll have subthemes such as billionaire romance or bad boy romance, and so on.

The best way to figure out what's selling is to look at Kindle's best sellers and look at the general theme. Note that fiction sells much more than nonfiction. The average nonfiction book you'll run into will have a BSR of 30,000 or so (if it sells well), but a fiction book will usually have a BSR of 100 or even 20.

Unsurprisingly, romance sells very well; the racier, the better. However, it's a crowded niche to break into, and it's tough to stand out. You'll have to work hard to drive traffic to your listing, as I'll explain shortly.

You can now figure out tropes by looking at book titles and figuring out what the target audience wants. Often, reading the book descriptions will reveal what the theme is. You can use the alphabet soup method to figure out tropes as well, but it doesn't work as well as nonfiction.

This is because people aren't searching for a particular keyword in fiction. They search for themes. So, you'll need to be creative when discovering new ones. The good news is that there are many YouTube channels out there that cover all aspects of indie publishing. Almost all of these authors are in the fiction space, so it's easy to get up-to-date information about what's working and what isn't.

Truth be told, finding tropes and themes in fiction is much easier than in nonfiction. However, standing out in vision is more demanding than with nonfiction. So, there's a trade-off. Start off with nonfiction first before branching out to fiction. This way, you'll build a good base for yourself before entering a more competitive space.

What to Avoid

You'll often see keywords pop up that yield very few results and a good number of best sellers. These keywords can mislead you, so be careful. Usually, they're misspelled, or they're the same as a best-selling book's title. For example, search for "intelligent investor," and you'll receive a small list of books, all of which are best sellers.

However, you'll notice that this keyword is almost precisely the same as *The Intelligent Investor* by Benjamin Graham, one of the most popular financial books ever written. A user that searches for this keyword isn't going to buy your title because they aren't searching for it.

So, stick to keywords that make sense, which isn't matching popular books. This applies to fiction as well. You're more likely to see keywords followed by character names or author names in a dream, for example, "billionaire romance Arthur" or something similar. These aren't good keywords since they indicate that the user is looking for something specific and is unlikely to click on your book listing.

Driving Traffic

The key to success in KDP is to drive traffic to your listing. Previously, Amazon used to direct a ton of organic traffic to book listings, but these days, it's impossible to rely on Amazon to drive traffic to your book organically. You'll have to pay for traffic from Amazon using their ads system, Amazon Advertising.

The problem with Amazon Advertising is that it's an expensive system to use, and your profit margins will be drawn thin. Therefore, it's best to create a system that drives traffic to your books organically. This way, you'll be in complete control of your audience and won't have to rely on Amazon to drive traffic to your readers.

Best of all, it'll give you a great platform from which you can publish your own books through your website and keep all of the money you make, instead of giving Amazon the majority of your royalties.

Here's a step-by-step process to build a traffic machine.

Step One—Website

To successfully generate traffic, you need a website. There's no way around this, unfortunately. You'll read a lot about people using social media as their sole traffic generation method, but this isn't sustainable in the long run. To succeed, you need a brand.

To create a brand, you need to focus on two things. The first is your name as the author, and the second is your series' name. Anything that gets people to recognize you and helps you stand out can be your brand. For example, Sherlock Holmes is a brand, as is Dan Brown. The first is a character, and the second is an author.

You don't have to use your real name. A pen name will do the trick as well. Given that the best-selling stuff in fiction tends to be salacious material, it's probably a good idea to use a pen name. Either way, pick a name and a catchy title for your book.

Your book needs to be a part of a series. You could break your series up into books within nonfiction aimed at the beginner, intermediate, and advanced readers. If you're publishing a series of vegan cookbooks, you could have a vegan breakfast cookbook, vegan lunch and dinner, and a dessert cookbook. The choice is yours.

To determine a series structure for yourself, you can look at other titles and authors in your keyword to figure out how others break up their books. The great thing about a series is that it allows you to bundle your books together and sell them for a higher price than an individual book. You'll understand the significance of this when you learn about audiobooks shortly.

Once you have your series titles figured out, it's time to create your website. It doesn't have to be fancy. List your book information along with snippets of text next to each title. If you're publishing just one title at first, then it's OK to list just that one, along with a placeholder indicating that other tags are releasing soon.

Generally, you want to release nonfiction series titles within a month of one another. The timeline varies with fiction. A lot depends on your book's size and on what note you left the previous book. If you left it on a cliffhanger, you could take a little time between books since people will be automatically engaged.

If you ended it without much of a bang, then you'll need to follow up with another book quickly. Some fiction writers churn books out every two weeks. These books are usually between 30,000-50,000 words long. The longer the book is, the more time you can take. Aim to release a book every month for safety's sake and seek your audience's feedback.

It's imperative that you set up a newsletter on your website. This newsletter will allow you to stay in touch with your readers and will allow you to announce new releases and build enthusiasm for your next book. Your email list is the most essential part of your marketing plan, so make sure it's in place. Do not underestimate its power.

Step Two—Find an Audience

The next step is perhaps the toughest for nonfiction writers but is easy for fiction publishers. Nonfiction audiences reside in different places. If you're publishing books on technical subjects such as coding or business productivity, then a social media network such as LinkedIn is a great option.

Hobbies tend to have a good number of Facebook groups dedicated to them, and you can publicize your book there as well. Note that you won't have your book entirely written at this point, so it's a good idea to have a snippet ready. Ensure you're adding value to the group and aren't spamming people with your information.

Urge people to sign up for your newsletter on your website to stay in touch. You can also mention that you're looking for people to join your ARC (Advance Reader Copy) team. I'll explain what this is short. For now, understand that readers are usually enthusiastic about joining an ARC team, and you're more likely to receive signups by doing this.

Instagram accounts dedicated to your niche are also a good way of receiving signups. You'll have to pay for a shout-out, but it's worth it in the long run. You can also convince the person running the account to subscribe to your list and become an ARC member. You can similarly use YouTube.

The idea at this stage is to get as many people as possible to sign up for your newsletter. Facebook groups are dedicated to publicizing new authors in specific genres, so join those groups as well. Do not pay for publicity at this stage. You'll find many websites that claim to have access to thousands of potential readers. Many beginner authors and publishers pay for these services.

However, they neglect that these readers will purchase books from brands they're familiar with. If they don't know who you are, no amount of persuading can help you. Therefore, it's best to build a brand first and use these services later.

Reddit is another option you can explore. However, the user base on Reddit is susceptible to promotion, so make sure you're an active member of those communities before you start pushing your books on them. Always follow community guidelines, and you'll be fine. This applies to all social media platforms in general.

Step Three—Build Your ARC

Your ARC team is the most critical component of your marketing strategy. Your ARC team's members are the ones who will leave you your first few reviews when you launch your book. Thoughts are all critical to the Amazon algorithm. Without reviews, you'll find your book dropping in the listings, and you won't be able to sustain any sort of momentum.

Once you've built a sizable audience dedicated to your work, you won't have to worry too much about what the algorithm does.

However, initially, you'll have to rely on it to bring in people who haven't heard of you before. This is how you'll build your user base and get even more people to sign up for your email newsletter.

Your ARC team will receive advance copies of your book, and upon release, will leave reviews. They'll have to explicitly mention that they were given advance copies of your book in their reviews. This is following Amazon's terms of service. Aim to build your ARC list to at least 50 people.

If this sounds like a lot, then don't worry. You'll find that most people will be enthusiastic about signing up as long as you're fishing in the right places. Another option you have for finding ARC members is to sort through the reviews of other books in your genre and notice who leaves the most reviews. You can contact them on Amazon and ask them if they'd like to be a part of your list.

Many Facebook groups are dedicated to ARC group formation, with people looking to join these lists. Maintain a spreadsheet of all the people on your list and mark the dates when they're supposed to leave their reviews.

For example, if you're planning on releasing your book on August 3rd, they would need to leave their reviews by August 5th at the latest. It's a good idea to maintain a separate email list or tag these subscribers with a label that shows they're an ARC member. Send them reminders two weeks, a week, and 24 hours before your book's release.

You need to track how many people respond to your emails and leave reviews. Drop the ones that aren't responsive—something else to watch out for his ARC members plagiarizing your work. Many ARC members are authors themselves, so you want to keep a sharp eye out for anyone copying your work. It's almost impossible to find everyone who does this, and the truth is told, few people plagiarize books like this, but it's wise to prevent this.

One way is to send out just a portion of your manuscript. Let them know it isn't the final version and that they'll receive free copies of the book once it's launched. Alternatively, you can offer them a discounted price. However, unless you're famous or well established, a free copy works best.

Monitor your ARC members' activity regularly, and don't hesitate to drop someone who isn't pulling their weight.

Step Four—Write and Design

This step should be conducted parallel with the previous one. You'll have to work on your marketing channels in parallel with writing your book. Make sure it's well-edited and doesn't have any typesetting errors. Also, leave a link at the beginning of your book for people to subscribe to your email list. Something that trips up newbie authors is that they don't design and format their books well.

To succeed on Amazon, you need to publish across three formats. You'll need to publish it as an ebook, a paperback, and an audiobook. Paperbacks are not always necessary. For example, if your genre is erotic, it's unlikely anyone will buy a print version of your book. However, you'll have to have an ebook and audiobook at the very least.

There are many services on websites such as Upwork and Fiverr that offer to format your book correctly. Hire a freelancer to design your ebook cover and convert it to a paperback and audiobook cover as well. Usually, the same person can format your book for ebook and paperback. All you'll need to do is hand over the Microsoft Word file to them.

You'll receive the following documents/files at the end of this process:

1. Formatted ebook (usually a .mobi file)
2. Ebook cover (jpeg or png file)
3. Formatted paperback manuscript (typically a 6-inch x 9-inch format as a docx file)
4. Formatted paperback cover (pdf)
5. Audiobook cover (jpeg)

If you're not publishing a paperback, you can ignore points three and four in the list above. Set your launch date and all that you need to do now is upload the book to KDP's backend, and you're all set.

When uploading your book, the system will guide you through the process. It's self-explanatory for the most part. You'll need to enter keywords that will help people find your book. Refer back to your keyword research process to identify relevant keywords you can use. Remember that you'll have to use trope names or theme names instead of actual keywords for fiction books.

Step Five —Release an Audiobook

This step is one of the most important ones you can undertake. I'll explain this in detail in a later section in this chapter. For now, let's look at the next step.

Step Six—Repeat

Once you've released your book, monitor the sales and reviews you receive. It's a good idea to publicize your book's release on your groups and networks. Send a notification to your email list and monitor how your subscriber count grows. At this point, it's time to work on your next book.

Since this is a follow-up to your previous one, you'll need to carry the story or theme over. Let your email list know you're working on the next book. You can even send them little snippets, especially in the case of fiction, and build enthusiasm. It's also a good idea to ask your audience (via a poll or form) what they want to read about.

Nonfiction writers will find these polls especially helpful since they can tailor their content better. Remember to keep executing the previous steps. Don't slack off your marketing once you've reached a specific size. Always keep increasing your list size and keep growing your subscriber count.

In the beginning, you should consider running Amazon ads. Amazon is particularly partial to self-published authors that run ads. How ethical this practice is is up for debate. However, there's not much you can do about it. You can set up your ads on Amazon Marketplace by mentioning keywords and setting minimum bids. The best way to handle Amazon ads is to choose a small number of keywords that are exact matches to your book's genre and leave it at that.

Always pay attention to whether or not your ads are making you money. If an ad isn't earning you enough, stop it immediately. There's no reason to give Amazon more money than they're already making off your hard work.

Step Seven—Expand

This step only applies once you've established a decent following and aren't reliant on Amazon's ad system to generate views for your book. If your subscriber list is over 1,000 and you're receiving above-average engagement, then you can safely execute this step.

Other book publishing platforms such as Draft2Digital and Reedsy allow you to create your books. These platforms pay you more outstanding royalties. Another option is to host books on your own website and keep all of your money to yourself.

You can use your existing books to double your revenue by bundling all of your books into a single book, based on a series, and offer the bundle at a higher price than a single book. Bundles work exceptionally well in nonfiction and will boost your earnings massively.

Lastly, consider translating your books into foreign languages, mainly Spanish and German. These markets are considerably large, and any book that does well in the English market will do well in these markets. Ensure you use reliable translation services since you don't want Amazon to ban you for poor content quality.

Once again, focus on expansion once you've established an excellent base for yourself. Before that, it really makes little sense to expand.

Audiobooks

Audiobook use is on the rise, and Amazon is one of the market's most prominent players through its Audible platform. In typical Amazon fashion, though, creators aren't really afforded many luxuries and have to adhere to standards or face lifetime bans. Something else to note is that ACX, Audible's back-end platform, is only available to US, Canada, and UK residents. It's not worth dealing with the intricacies of audiobook production by yourself since ACX's requirements can madden (*ACX Submission Requirements,* 2021). However, the platform makes it easy for you to hire producers.

Once you've released your ebook on KDP, you head over to ACX and log in using your KDP credentials. You'll have to "assert" your title by clicking the button labeled with that word. Once this is done, you'll enter all relevant details and will have a chance to either hire a producer directly or host an audition.

It's usually common to pay $50 per finished audio hour for a producer. You can review auditions and hire a producer. Send the manuscript over to the producer, and they'll narrate your book by

chapter and post the files on ACX. You can download these files for later use as well. Another option is to hire a producer through a freelance platform and upload the finished files to ACX. As long as the formatting is correct, you won't have any issues.

Once the book is produced, you'll face the most maddening part of the process. This is ACX's quality assurance process, which takes close to forever. That's not an exaggeration. Typically, new authors face approval times of close to three months and no amount of emailing ACX helps. They move at their own pace, and more likely, you'll be hit with a notice saying your files aren't up to scratch at the end of the three months.

This is where it helps to hire a narrator on the ACX platform since you can hold them accountable. Consider paying more to avoid having to upload everything again and wait for another three months for approval. Now, if you're on a tight publishing schedule, these lengthy wait times don't work.

It's best to choose an alternate platform to publish your audiobook. The best alternate platform is Findaway Voices, where you can upload your audiobook and have it approved in as

little as 48 hours. This coincides nicely with your ebook release. You can't publish a Findaway link in your ebook manuscript, but you can mention it as a text.

Also, notify your email subscribers that an audiobook is available on that platform and not on ACX as yet. Both ACX and funds will price your book according to its length. The longer your book is, the higher its price. Therefore, bundles are a money machine in audiobooks since listeners pay based on finished audio hours.

It's best to rely on ACX as little as possible. However, you can't ignore it since Amazon's traffic is enormous, and their cross-promotion on your book's listing page helps drive sales. Expand to other audiobook platforms as quickly as possible and avoid relying on ACX's notoriously hopeless customer service.

How Passive Is It?

Reading all of this, you might well wonder how passive all of this is? Truth be told, it isn't passive in the beginning. However, once you have five to ten books under your brand, you'll find that the machine will sustain itself. As word spreads of your books' quality, Amazon's algorithm will notice your sales are high and will promote your books up the product listings by themselves.

The key is to scale as quickly as possible to hit a decent passive income figure every month. Take your time building a quality content machine, and don't rush through the marketing process. You'll reap the rewards in due course.

Chapter 9: Money-Making Websites

You've already learned that starting a blog or a content channel and monetizing it via affiliate marketing is an excellent way of making passive income. However, the process takes time, and you'll have to be really motivated to continue working on the website. What if you could shortcut the process and start earning money with a bit of financial investment upfront?

Many websites are up for sale, and how you can monetize your content are many. This chapter will help you learn about buying sites (or blogs) ready to make money or are already earning money.

I'll also discuss monetizing these sites, apart from affiliate marketing. Note that you can use these methods as standalone strategies as well. However, they work best when backed up by a website that is earning money, to begin with.

Buying Websites

A decade ago, a website wasn't viewed as a serious business. Sure, people earned money from their websites, but it was considered a niche thing and not a mainstream business. These days, with every business having an online presence, a website is essentially a business. You must treat one.

Having established that ground rule, you'll find that there are many businesses up for sale across every niche you can think of. You'll find sites that have been monetized using Amazon affiliate links through ad networks (where the website owner gets paid to host ads), through courses, and other avenues.

You need to have a thorough review process that you can use to quickly identify a good business to buy. The price of these websites depends on the money they earn every month. Typically, you'll find that these websites yield a high percentage. It isn't unusual to see yields of 30% or greater.

However, understand that these yields are sustainable only through continued work. It isn't as if you can buy a website and then forget about it. You'll have to put the work in and manage the site. Like I said, you're buying a business, so you'll need to dedicate some amount of time to maintain it. When done right, though, you'll find that increasing the website's revenues will exponentially increase the return on your investment and will be disconnected from the time you spend developing it.

Needless to say, since you're buying someone else's business, you'll need to have money in the bank. At the very least, aim to have $5,000 of capital. Note that not all of this money should buy a website. You'll need spare capital to run the business successfully.

Let's look at the first factor you should evaluate.

Niche

The website's niche is the most important thing to begin with. While the niche might be lucrative, it's helpful to evaluate whether there's anything in there that interests you. For example, you might look at purchasing an essential oils website for $2,500 that earns $88 per month.

That's a handy 42% yield per year. While the money is good in terms of percentages, the amount doesn't really get measurable results. Are you willing to build the website up and growing its audience? Do you have enough interest in the niche to create new content (or enough money to pay someone to do so) and increase your revenues?

If you aren't interested in the niche, you'll be dealing with a headache, no matter how good your yield is. However, if the yield amount is high, the niche might not matter to you. The same website sells for $25,000 and generates $880 per month.

That's a substantial amount of cash that can cover significant expenses. Despite the niche not being to your liking, this might be an excellent investment for you. The compensation you receive makes up for the lack of interest you have in the niche.

An online business goes up for sale more often than not because something fundamental to it has changed. It could either be traffic-related or that the owner has lost interest. Either way, you're going to have to brainstorm ways of continuing the momentum the business has built up.

Therefore, prepare to spend some time and money on it. Consequently, it helps choose a niche you're passionate about or knowledgeable in. The less intense you are about that niche, the more attention you ought to pay to how much you'll earn every month and how much you'll need to spend to keep the ball rolling.

Traffic

Traffic is the lifeblood of every business, and it's also one of the primary reasons a company goes up for sale. You want to see a website garner traffic through organic search as much as possible. Often, you'll find websites that gain a huge percentage of their traffic through social media.

This leaves them vulnerable to algorithm changes. For example, you'll currently find many websites that receive close to 40% of their traffic from Pinterest up for sale. This isn't an accident. Pinterest was famous for directing vast amounts of organic traffic to content creators until recently.

However, recent algorithm changes have pushed users towards paid ads, and as a result, many websites have witnessed significant drops in their traffic numbers. Stay away from any listing that depends on social media, and stick to those with a good amount of organic and direct traffic.

Backlinks

Technically, Backlinks are a part of the traffic equation, but they deserve their own section since organic traffic can be sabotaged. Backlinking used to present a loophole to take advantage of Google's algorithm. The way it worked was to use private blog networks (PBNs) to refer traffic to the primary site.

Let's say you set up a website around dog toys. You could then create a website centered on dog training and leave a link in all of your posts to the toys' website. Next, you could create another website centered on pet food and leave a link to the toys' website. Creating multiple websites like this would fool Google into thinking that many websites are linking to your primary website, and therefore, it must be credible.

The result was a boost in search engine optimization (SEO) rankings. However, Google's algorithm has caught on to the fact that PBNs are used extensively, and many website owners who used this strategy have been consistently penalized with every algorithm update. These days, Google doesn't announce updates to its algorithm and instead issues more minor updates. The result is a slow death instead of a sudden change in traffic.

If you see any listing that contains or mentions a PBN, it's best to stay away from it. It's not a sustainable way of earning traffic, and eventually, you'll lose your organic search position.

Reason for Selling

As a rule of thumb, the more expensive the listing is, the more credible it is. An expensive listing has a proper business attached to it, with employees and supply channels. A less expensive listing requires more research since its profitability depends on how it has gained traffic. There are simply fewer pillars supporting it.

It's helpful to talk to the seller and determine their selling reason. Most sellers won't agree to this upfront. However, you can always ask them via email for their reason for selling. If a seller isn't upfront with you about their reasoning or avoids the question, walk away from the deal.

The most common reason you'll receive is that the seller has other projects or is uninterested in the primary website. Whatever their reason is, you want to get a feel for who they are before paying them money.

Value Add

An important question to ask yourself is whether the business has maxed out its growth potential or whether there's still room to expand. Usually, expansion involves investing more money and growing the business. However, it's easy to leverage an existing audience and expand the business, thereby increasing your chances of increasing your passive income potential exponentially.

You'll find many websites that have reached the peak of their monetization ability and can't sustain their earnings. This doesn't mean that every website close to its monetization peak is a lousy bet. It's just that the income streams should be sustainable.

For example, many niche websites and blogs use Amazon affiliates to earn income. The problem with this income stream is that Amazon is notorious for changing its commissions based on what it wants to sell on its platform. If a niche website is earning a lot of money thanks to high affiliate commissions, it's a good idea to halve those commissions and test how much money it can reach.

Tailor your offer price accordingly. Aim for a yield of at least 25% after adjusting the income. If the seller disagrees, walk away. After all, it's not like you need to invest in that business.

Increasing Revenues

There are different ways of increasing the revenues of an existing website. However, a few methods have proved to be the ones with the most passive income potential. Note that these methods can income-earning avenues by themselves. However, they're best used when backed by a website.

Create a Course

Creating a course is one of the easiest ways of generating passive income. All you need to do is spend time initially creating a system, and once you put it up for sale, it continues to develop money for you with minimal marketing effort. Of course, this doesn't mean you can create just about any system and expect it to sell well.

You'll have to add value to your audience and give them what they want. When paired with a website, a course can be an excellent passive income source since you'll already have a captive audience. The best part of creating a system is that you don't have to make yourself.

You can always hire someone to create a course on the topic and market it as an expert's view. For example, if you're selling essential oils to your customers, adding a lecture about meditation or healing naturally is a great way to boost your website's content. You can also add exercise plans or meal plans and boost earnings that way.

The key is to add value at all times. If you're launching a standalone course, then you can choose to upload your content to websites such as Udemy that can host your system for free. You'll need to spend time and money marketing your course through social media and other online channels. Using influencer marketing (where you pay an influencer to feature your course and review it) is a powerful way of getting the message out to your intended audience.

Creating an App

This technique doesn't work for all websites, but monetizing your website through an app can make sense in specific niches. If your blog or website is in the education niche, then creating an app can significantly increase customer loyalty and generate another income stream.

The good news is that you don't need any coding skills to successfully create an app. You can use platforms such as Appy Pie to point and click your way to a fantastic app. You can create gated content (content behind a paywall), or you can open your app up to ads much like you would your website to keep it free and earn money from your users.

Most website owners underestimate how helpful adding an app can be. Sticking with the previous natural oils website example, at first glance, you'd think that there isn't much of an opportunity to develop an app. However, what if you could create an app that delivers motivational quotes every morning (in a spiritual vein)?

What if you extended that app and turned it into a meditation app with subscriptions (another excellent passive income technique)? You might wonder where you'll create meditation scripts from. Well, how about you type *10-minute meditation* into YouTube and recreate those scripts using royalty-free music?

The limits are endless! All you need to do is think outside the box. Value-adding your existing website by creating new products and marketing them to your existing audience is an excellent way of creating more passive income. Best of all, it takes a one-time effort, and you're all set.

If you're thinking of launching a standalone app, this is a great idea as well. It pays to look at the Apple and Google Play stores to see what kind of apps sell well. However, much like launching a standalone course, you'll need to figure out how you can drive people to your app.

If you need to spend money driving traffic to an app, you might as well create a business or buy one and use that audience to drive downloads. It just makes more sense. You won't have to reinvent the wheel trying to find an audience. Just buy one and monetize them through value-addition.

Social Media Influencing

Influencers come under a ton of flak these days, but the business model isn't completely dead or as exploitive as is often suggested. Besides, there are many ways of becoming a social media influencer. Ask an online business novice what they think an influencer is, and they'll most probably envision an obnoxious person posing shirtless (or in a bikini) in some tropical paradise.

Sure, that's one kind of influencer. However, you can be a travel influencer and simply post pretty pictures of exotic destinations. You can be a humor influencer and report funny videos. You can be a pet niche influencer by posting cute dog and kitten videos. (There are never enough!)

My point is that just like how most people underestimate the power of an app to increase their revenues, they probably underestimate how influential their business can be. Let's stick with the natural oils theme again. It's easy to turn that business into a wellness-themed store that promotes natural, healthy living.

You can monetize Instagram by posting pictures of Yoga workouts and healthy food choices. Throw in a few of your own product pictures for good measure. Eventually, you could partner with another influencer and sell their products for a commission. Hello, affiliate marketing!

All of this sounds like a lot of work, but as you begin to stretch your legs in your business, you'll dream up income opportunities yourself. Once that happens, the sky's the limit! You can try to become an influencer by yourself, without a business audience's backing.

However, it takes time. This isn't to say that it's a dead-end prospect. It's just that you need to be realistic about the kind of effort it'll take. Remember that you can be an influencer on any social media platform, not just Instagram. You can be an influencer on Twitter or YouTube as well. Facebook isn't of much use since that platform is only interested in squeezing users for money.

With the right strategies, you can become an influencer and begin to earn passive income through shout-outs or affiliate marketing. As always, it's best to approach it with the power of a captive business audience behind your back.

Chapter 10: Invest in a Business

I nvesting in a business sounds very complicated, as if it's something that only the most sophisticated of players should undertake. Well, there is some truth to this. However, who's to say that you aren't sophisticated enough to invest money in a business? Most of us underestimate our business chops.

This is because we overcomplicate things and chase money. Instead, we should be pursuing opportunities we're good at. This is where we have an edge, and it makes the most sense to deploy more excellent resources there. If a friend approaches you with the intent of getting you to invest in their furniture business, ask yourself whether you know anything about furniture.

Do you know what the business is like, and can you understand its economics after your friend explains everything to you? Do you trust them entirely as a person? These critical questions are often left by the wayside in the pursuit of money. Becoming a silent partner in a private business is a great way to earn passive income since you get to make money and let others do the work.

Debt Versus Equity

When you give someone money to invest in their business, you can do this in two ways. You can buy equity in their business or lend them the money (this is called debt financing.) When you buy equity, you're buying shares in their business much as you would with any company on the stock exchange through a broker.

Debt financing involves earning interest payments over a term. In this scenario, you're lending them money at a specific interest rate and will receive the principal back after a certain period. In most traditional private business investments, debt financing isn't offered. Even if the founders typically offer convertible debt, which means after some point, the debt gets converted to equity.

However, one arena where debt financing is prevalent is real estate. Here, there's almost no mention of equity since everyone is chasing funding. You can make debt financing in real estate work for you a few ways.

Hard Money Loans

A hard money lender provides bridge financing to real estate investors. Remember what bridge financing is? It's the kind of financing extended to real estate investors looking to control distressed properties. Many experienced real estate investors transition to the other side and offer financing since the cash flow is steady and the risk is a lot less.

Typically, a hard money lender offers more excellent interest rates than prevailing market rates. The risk is offset by the fact that properties they're financing are in poor condition, and they rely on the rehabber's expertise to execute a successful flip. When you consider that the average hard money lender extends interest rates of 12% or more, you can see the appeal in the business.

To succeed as a hard money lender, you need to register as a business and obtain the necessary licensing. There is a business setup cost involved, but this is offset by the amount of money you'll earn. You'll have to conduct due diligence before extending cash to someone. However, once the deal is signed, all you need to do is collect interest payments.

If the borrower defaults on payments, you can foreclose and gain control of the property. This may or may not be to your liking. The best way forward in this situation is to partner with a property flipper and assume equity in the deal so you can realize a profit.

However, becoming a hard money lender is a pretty passive way of collecting passive income without assuming property ownership risks. The flip side is that you need significant amounts of money in the bank, usually mid-six figures, to be taken seriously.

If you have that sort of cash lying around, you can start networking in your local real estate club and start cutting deals.

Mortgage Notes

Hard money lending requires you to have a significant amount of capital. What if you could replicate the business model with far less money? Well, that's where a mortgage note or m-note comes into the picture. A mortgage note represents the unpaid portion of a mortgage. Typically, if a borrower cannot repay the mortgage, the bank sells that mortgage on the open market to private investors. After all, they aren't in the business of homeownership.

Private investors can buy these notes and gain authority over the property. It's essential to recognize that a message can represent a first or second lien over a property. If you buy a second lien (which is junior to a first lien), you're not going to be able to take possession of the property.

In most cases, m-note investors renegotiate payments with borrowers and work payment plans to keep everyone happy. The bank sells you the notes at a steep discount since they want to clear those assets off their books and recover a portion of their money.

You can find great deals on m-notes at places like Paperstac and BankProspector. Flip is also an excellent resource that connects real estate investors with financing options. M-notes are just one kind of investment opportunity available there. You can fund a flip or rehab project as well on that platform.

Before diving into m-note investing, make sure you're aware of the worst-case scenarios. In this case, the worst possible method for you will be if the borrower doesn't pay you back and you're stuck with a property that cannot be sold at any cost. Therefore, the thing to do is to avoid properties that are complete duds.

It's also a good idea to avoid vacant lots or raw land lots. These don't sell quickly, and you'll be stuck with a piece of land for an extended period. Buying farmland is a significant investment, but that's not the kind of land you'll see attached to m-notes. They'll usually be empty patches of land stuck between two developments that are too small to be developed.

Overall, there are excellent opportunities to be a silent partner in a private business and a real estate opportunity. You will need a good amount of capital to make these opportunities work, except in the case of mortgage notes, where you can get started with as little as $5,000.Best of all, these opportunities are amongst the most passive and lucrative ones out there. It takes time to build up to these opportunities, so be patient and not rush the process.

Conclusion

P assive income is a great way to boost your wealth, but it isn't as if it's free money. You'll need to work for it and plan in advance. The methods I've given you in this book are excellent ways of building passive income, but all of them vary in terms of the activity required upfront and the degree of passivity you can expect.

All of them can be turned entirely passive by hiring someone to run the venture for you (even stock investing), but this will cost you money, and you'll need to have a ton of capital, usually seven figures. Therefore, don't be in a rush to turn everything completely passive. Take your time with these income streams and choose the ones that appeal to you.

You'll read a lot about how millionaires have seven streams of income and so on, and you will be tempted to build seven streams using these opportunities. First off, the notion that you need seven income streams to get rich is unvarnished nonsense. Most billionaires have just one stream of income. Bill Gates makes his money through Microsoft, Jeff Bezos through Amazon, and Mark Zuckerberg through Facebook.

These people didn't go around trying to create seven sources of income. Instead, they focused on what they were good at and created enough wealth to generate passive income investments. Even then, it's hard to imagine that Jeff Bezos or Mark Cuban make more money through passive income than through their active sources of income.

This is often the reality of passive income. It's tough to completely replace your active income with passive income without assuming high debt levels. Your day job is still essential, and it

Conclusion

gives you the security you need to build other streams of income. Many people enter the world of passive income to quit their day job and so on. It's possible to earn enough money to replace your day job, but don't assume that you'll do it overnight. Also, don't make the mistake of thinking that you won't need to work to create passive income. As you've seen, almost all of these methods require you to work hard and then reap the rewards of your labor.

Therefore, take it easy and don't fall for get-rich-quick schemes that tell you you're a loser if you work for a boss. Be patient and get rich slowly. It's the only way to get rich, and best of all, it doesn't take anywhere near as much time as you might imagine.

I'm optimistic that this book has given you many insights into the passive income creation process and that your mind must be buzzing with ideas now. Let me know what you think by leaving me a review.

I wish you all the luck in the world and hope to hear about your growing passive income over the next few years!

References

5 Ways to Make Money Renting Out Your Car. (2021, January 12). Well Kept Wallet. https://wellkeptwallet.com/make-money-renting-out-car/

ACX Submission Requirements. (2021, March 24). Www.acx.com. https://www.acx.com/help/acx-audio-submission-requirements/201456300

Dweck, C. S. (2006). Mindset: The New Psychology of Success. Ballantine Books.

Graham, B. (1985). The Intelligent Investor: A Book of Practical Counsel. Harper & Row.

Hanson, R., & Mendius, R. (2009). Buddha's Brain: The Practical Neuroscience of Happiness, Love & Wisdom. New Harbinger Publications.

Hoffower, H. (2021, March 24). Financial Happiness Starts at $85,000 per Year. Business Insider. https://www.businessinsider.com/personal-finance/money-buys-happiness-depending-on-income-level-2021-1?r=US&IR=T#:~:text=Americans%20earning%20more%20than%20%2485%2C000

References

Mischel, W. (2014). The Marshmallow Test: Mastering Self-Control. Little, Brown And Company.

Patel, N. (2019, February 15). How Loading Time Affects Your Bottom Line. Neil Patel. https://neilpatel.com/blog/loading-time/

Popova, M. (2016, January 27). Mozart's Daily Routine. Brain Pickings. https://www.brainpickings.org/2016/01/27/mozart-daily-routine/

Schroeder, A. (2009). The Snowball: Warren Buffett and the Business of Life. Bantam Books.

Scott, J. (2015). The Book on Estimating Rehab Costs: The Investor's Guide to Defining Your Renovation Plan, Building Your Budget, and Knowing Exactly How Much It All Costs. Lish Marketing, Llc.

All images from Pixabay

Made in the USA
Las Vegas, NV
29 July 2021